THE · BOOK

SALADS

THE   BOOK   OF

SALADS

LORNA RHODES

Photography by
Sue Jorgensen,
assisted by Des Adams

HPBooks
a division of
PRICE STERN SLOAN

ANOTHER BEST SELLING VOLUME FROM HPBOOKS

Published by HPBooks
A division of Price Stern Sloan, Inc.
11150 Olympic Boulevard,
Los Angeles, C   90064

10 9 8 7 6 5

By arrangement with Salamander Books Ltd. and Merehurst Press,
London.

©Salamander Books Ltd., 1988

This book was created by Merehurst Limited
5, Great James Street, London WCIN 3DA

Designer: Roger Daniels
Home Economist: Lorna Rhodes
Photographer: Sue Jorgensen, assisted by: Des Adams
Color separation: Kentscan Limited
Printed in Belgium by Proost International Book Production,
Turnhout

Library of Congress Cataloging-in-Publication Data

Rhodes, Lorna
    Book of salads.

    Includes Index.
    1. Salads   I. Title.
TX740.M626 1988   641.8'3   88-21327
ISBN0-89586-791-5 (pbk.)

CONTENTS

INTRODUCTION

A salad can be different each time it is made: the enormous variety of produce available all year round contributes to an ever-changing combination of colors, textures and flavors. And thanks to improved international distribution, many supermarkets now stock the more exotic fruits and vegetables, making it easy to create unusual and appealing salads for any occasion—buffet, formal dinner, family lunch or casual picnic.

Salads are the heart of healthful eating, providing a rich source of many important vitamins and minerals. But to make the best salads, you must start with the best ingredients: fresh, top-quality produce, lean meats and poultry, low-calorie seafood, and wholesome pasta, grains and legumes.

This book offers over 100 salad recipes, all illustrated with beautiful color photographs. There are simple, familiar favorites—tossed green salads, potato salads, Waldorf salad—as well as more unusual partnerships featuring sweet, colorful tropical fruits or even flowers. There are first courses, side dishes and entrées, including the sophisticated new *salades tièdes* that combine warm ingredients with cold ones for a delightful contrast. Above all, there is variety— you will find salads to suit any taste and any season.

GLOSSARY OF SALAD GREENS

Described below are some of the best greens for salads. For the most interesting flavor, you'll want to combinc two or more types whenever possible. Buy only the freshest greens: the leaves should be crisp and clean, with a good color.

Belgian endive has slender, spear-shaped heads tightly packed with white or palest yellow leaves that can be used whole or chopped. Bitter in flavor, endive is often combined with fruits in salads.

Bibb resembles butter lettuce, but its outer leaves are crisper and frillier.

Butter lettuce looks something like a small, soft cabbage. Its tender, mild-tasting leaves are darker green on the outside of the head, paler in the center.

Chicory (frisé, curly endive) grows in large, very frilly heads that are dark green outside, pale yellow within. Crisp in texture and slightly bitter in flavor, it is often mixed with other greens.

Chinese cabbage (cclcry cabbage, napa cabbage) has firm, elongated heads that resemble a fat romaine lettuce. The crinkly, pale-green-to-white leaves are sweet and juicy, milder tasting than typical head cabbage.

Escarole (batavia, broad-leafed endive) has broader, less curly leaves than chicory, but it too has a bitter flavor.

Iceberg is a very crisp, very pale green lettuce available all year round. The leaves are so tightly packed it is difficult to separate them. Iceberg is often chopped, shredded or cut into wedges.

Leaf lettuce has big, frilly, tender leaves that grow in loose heads. Most markets sell both red and green varieties of this mild-tasting lettuce.

Lizzle Gem. See *Romaine*.

Lollo rosso has red-edged, very frizzy leaves that make a pretty addition to the salad bowl.

Mâche (lamb's lettuce, corn salad) is easily recognized by its clusters of dark green, tongue-shaped leaves. It's another slightly bitter green.

Oak leaf lettuce, also known as red salad bowl lettuce, has floppy leaves—purplish red on the outside, dark green in the center. As the name indicates, they're shaped like oak leaves.

Radicchio (red chicory) looks like a large, reddish-purple Brussels sprout and tastes much like Belgian endive. Its wonderful color brightens up salads.

Romaine (cos) is a favorite throughout the Mediterranean. Its long, spear-shaped leaves are crisp and deep green. **Little Gem** is a miniature romaine, just 5 inches long; it is paler in color than the full-sized lettuce.

Spinach, especially useful in warm salads, provides a nice contrast to sharper flavors.

PREPARING
—— GREENS ——

Keep lettuces and other greens in a plastic bag or container in the crisper drawer of your refrigerator. Before using, separate and wash the leaves, discarding any that are yellow or wilted. To remove excess water, whirl the leaves in a salad spinner or pat them gently with cloth or paper towels. (Dry leaves stay crisp longer, and dressings will coat them more evenly.) Just before serving, tear (don't cut) the leaves into smaller pieces unless the recipe indicates otherwise; add the dressing, toss and serve.

—— DRESSINGS ——

A well-made dressing adds the final touch to any salad, enhancing and melding the fla-

vors. And like the salad itself, a good dressing should be made with top-quality ingredients —the best oils, vinegars and seasonings you can afford.

Dressings fall into two basic categories: vinaigrettes and mayonnaises. In this book, you'll also find a few dressings made with yogurt, sour cream and citrus juices.

The oil used in a dressing or mayonnaise greatly influences the flavor. Extra-virgin olive oil, a cold-pressed oil, is recommended in many cases, but it does have a strong, distinctive flavor. Should a less pronounced flavor be desired, use a lighter olive oil; or try sunflower, safflower or grapeseed oils, either on their own or mixed with olive oil.

A few recipes call for nut oils such as walnut and hazelnut oil, or for light or dark sesame oil (the darker oil has a stronger taste). Because these unusual oils can be rather overpowering when used alone, they are often mixed with sunflower oil. You might try using a blend of walnut and sunflower oils to make mayonnaise; to bring out the nut flavor, garnish the salad with freshly toasted walnuts.

Never use plain distilled vinegars to make dressings. Buy two or three good-quality vinegars such as sherry, cider and wine; or choose a few that are flavored with fruit, herbs or spices (tarragon vinegar is excellent). Fresh lemon juice can be used instead of vinegar.

For salad seasoning, use fine aromatic French mustard, sea salt and freshly ground black pepper. Or add an unusual touch by grinding a combination of colored peppercorns—black, white, pink, green—over your salad. Chopped fresh herbs such as parsley, basil, tarragon and chives add a marvelous touch, as do spices such as ground cumin, crushed chilies or fennel seeds.

Vinaigrette Dressing

1/2 teaspoon salt
Freshly ground black pepper to taste
1/2 teaspoon Dijon-style mustard
1/2 teaspoon sugar
2 tablespoons wine vinegar, herb-
    flavored vinegar or cider vinegar
6 tablespoons olive oil (less for a
    sharper-tasting dressing)

In a bowl, stir together salt, pepper, mustard, sugar and vinegar until salt and sugar are dissolved.

Pour in oil and whisk with a fork to combine.
(Or place all ingredients in a screw-top jar and shake until well blended.)
Makes about 1/2 cup.

Lemon Vinaigrette: Substitute fresh lemon juice for the vinegar.

Garlic Vinaigrette: Crush 1 or 2 garlic cloves and add to dressing.

Herb Vinaigrette: Add 1 to 2 tablespoons chopped fresh herbs, such as parsley, chervil, basil, tarragon or chives (or use a mixture).

Honey Vinaigrette: Substitute 1 teaspoon honey for the sugar.

Light Vinaigrette: Replace from half to all the olive oil with sunflower oil.

Mayonnaise

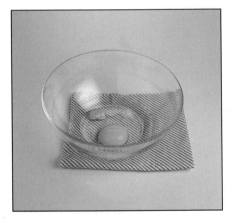

1 egg yolk
Pinch of salt
1/2 teaspoon Dijon-style mustard
2/3 cup olive oil
2 teaspoons white wine vinegar or lemon
   juice

To help prevent curdling, bring all ingredients to room temperature before
you begin. Place egg yolk in a bowl;
stand bowl on a cloth to keep it from
sliding about.

Whisk in salt and mustard. Whisking
constantly, begin to add oil—drop by
drop at first.

Increase to a steady trickle as the mayonnaise thickens. When all oil has been
added, beat in vinegar or lemon juice.
Correct seasoning, if necessary. If desired, thin mayonnaise with a little hot
water.
Makes about 2/3 cup.

Quick Blender Mayonnaise: Place egg yolk, salt and mustard in a blender and process 15 seconds. Then add oil—slowly at first, more quickly as mayonnaise thickens. Beat in vinegar or lemon juice, then correct seasoning.

Herb Mayonnaise: Add 2 tablespoons chopped fresh herbs, such as parsley, chives or tarragon (or use a mixture).

Garlic Mayonnaise (Aïoli): Crush 2 garlic cloves and add to egg yolk mixture before adding oil.

Light Mayonnaise: Replace from half to all the olive oil with sunflower oil. After mayonnaise has thickened, whisk in 2 tablespoons plain yogurt.

Yogurt Dressing

2/3 cup plain yogurt
2 tablespoons lemon juice
1 teaspoon Dijon-style mustard
1 teaspoon honey
Salt and freshly ground black pepper to taste

In a bowl, whisk together all ingredients until honey is thoroughly incorporated. Refrigerate before using.

Variations:

Herb Yogurt Dressing: Add 2 tablespoons chopped fresh herbs, such as tarragon, mint, parsley or chives (or use a mixture).

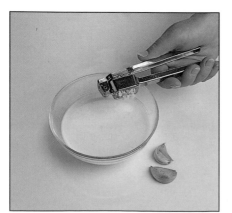

Garlic Yogurt Dressing: Add 1 garlic clove, crushed.

(This dressing is a low-calorie alternative to mayonnaise.) Makes 2/3 cup.

Oriental Dressing

6 tablespoons sunflower oil
4 teaspoons dark soy sauce
1 tablespoon dry sherry
1 garlic clove, crushed
1 teaspoon honey
1/2 teaspoon Chinese five-spice powder

In a bowl, whisk together all ingredients until well blended. Makes about 1/2 cup.

Variations:

Sesame Dressing: Follow preceding directions, but in place of listed ingredients use 2 tablespoons sunflower oil, 2 teaspoons dark sesame oil, 1 tablespoon light soy sauce, 1 teaspoon honey and 2 teaspoons rice vinegar. Makes about 1/3 cup.

Chinese Dressing: Follow preceding directions, but in place of listed ingredients use 2 tablespoons sunflower oil, 1 tablespoon light sesame oil, 1 tablespoon chili vinegar and 1 tablespoon light soy sauce. Makes about 1/3 cup.

Composed Salad

4 very small artichokes
4 oz. thin green beans, ends trimmed
Chicory leaves or lettuce leaves of your
   choice
1/2 recipe Garlic Vinaigrette, page 11
8 radishes, trimmed, cut into roses or
   fans, soaked in ice water to make
   them open
1 fennel bulb, trimmed, thinly sliced (reserve some of feathery leaves for garnish)
2 medium carrots, cut into long, thin
   shreds
1 recipe Garlic Mayonnaise, page 13

Trim stalks from artichokes. In a deep
saucepan, bring about 2 quarts water to
a boil. Add artichokes; reduce heat,
cover and simmer briskly about 20
minutes or until tender. Drain and let
cool. Cook beans in boiling water 3 minutes or just until bright green. Drain

and let cool. To assemble salads, arrange chicory or lettuce leaves on 1 side
of each of 4 plates. Remove some of
outer leaves from artichokes and fan
them out on other side of each plate.
Then cut artichokes in half and remove
fuzzy choke; place 2 artichoke halves,
cut side up, alongside artichoke leaves
on each plate. Spoon a little Garlic
Vinaigrette into each artichoke. Attractively arrange beans, radishes, fennel
and its leaves, add carrots on plates.
Serve Garlic Mayonnaise on the side.
Makes 4 servings.

Variations: Use any appealing ingredients you have on hand, such as
hard-cooked quail eggs, canned or
cooked miniature corn on the cob,
grated jicama, celery slices or cooked
green lima or fava beans.

Ceviche

1 lb. firm white-fleshed fish fillets, such as cod, lemon sole, halibut or sea bass, skinned
Juice of 5 limes (about 2/3 cup)
2 tablespoons olive oil
2 garlic cloves, finely chopped
3 tomatoes, peeled, seeded, chopped
1 small fresh green chili, seeded, finely chopped
1 small onion, finely chopped
12 to 16 green olives
2 tablespoons chopped fresh cilantro (coriander)
Salt and black pepper to taste
1/2 avocado
1 lime, sliced
Fresh cilantro (coriander) sprigs

Cut fish into thin slices or small chunks and place in a glass dish. Pour lime juice over fish. Cover and refrigerate 24 hours, stirring occasionally. Heat oil in a medium skillet, add garlic and cook just until it begins to turn pale gold. Remove from heat and let cool; then stir in tomatoes, chili, onion, olives and chopped cilantro. Season with salt and pepper. Drain marinated fish and add it to sauce. Mix well; cover and refrigerate. To serve, divide fish mixture among 4 dishes. Pit, peel and slice avocado. Garnish each portion with avocado, lime slices and cilantro sprigs; then serve at once. Makes 4 servings.

Seafood in Wine Jelly

1 (6-oz.) salmon steak, cut in half
12 small or 6 medium scallops
1-1/2 cups dry white wine
1 bay leaf
6 whole black peppercorns
2 large onion slices
Salt to taste
1 (1/4-oz.) envelope unflavored gelatin
1 cup bottled clam juice
6 oz. shelled, deveined cooked shrimp
Fresh dill sprigs
1 tablespoon olive oil
1 shallot, chopped
Pinch of saffron threads
3 tablespoons whipping cream

Place salmon and scallops in a medium saucepan and add 2/3 cup wine, bay leaf, peppercorns and onion slices. Season with salt. Bring to a boil; reduce heat, cover and simmer 5 to 6 minutes or until seafood is opaque throughout. Let cool in cooking liquid. Meanwhile, in a small saucepan, sprinkle gelatin over 1/2 cup clam juice and let stand about 5 minutes or until spongy. Then stir over low heat until gelatin is dissolved. Add remaining 1/2 cup clam juice and remaining wine, then spoon 1 tablespoon of the mixture into each of 6 oval 1/2-cup molds. Refrigerate until set. Lift salmon and scallops from pan; strain and reserve cooking liquid. Cut salmon into small pieces, discarding skin and bones. Slice scallops. Layer all salmon and scallops and about half the shrimp in molds, adding little dill sprigs between layers and pouring in a little gelatin mixture as the layers build up. When molds are full, refrigerate until set. Also refrigerate remaining shrimp and reserved cooking liquid. Heat oil in a small saucepan; add shallot and cook 2 minutes. Add reserved cooking liquid from fish; simmer 5 minutes. Place saffron in a bowl, pour hot shallot mixture over it and let cool. To unmold jellies, dip each mold up to rim in a bowl of hot water for a few seconds; invert onto a plate and lift off mold. Strain saffron mixture and whisk in cream; pour cream mixture around jellies. Garnish with dill sprigs and remaining shrimp. Makes 6 servings.

Caesar Salad

2 garlic cloves, peeled
6 tablespoons olive oil
4 thick slices bread, crusts removed
1 head romaine lettuce
6 flat anchovy fillets, chopped
1/4 cup freshly grated Parmesan cheese
(3/4 oz.)
Soft Egg Dressing, see below

Soft Egg Dressing:
1 egg
5 teaspoons lemon juice
3 tablespoons olive oil
1 teaspoon Worcestershire sauce
1/4 teaspoon Dijon-style mustard
Salt and black pepper to taste

To make garlic oil, cut each garlic clove in half. Place garlic and oil in a cup and let stand 1 hour; remove garlic. Cut bread slices into squares. Heat garlic oil in a skillet, add bread squares and cook until crisp and golden, turning frequently. Lift out and drain on paper towels. To assemble salad, tear most of lettuce into large pieces; reserve a few whole inner leaves and arrange them around edge of a salad bowl. Put torn lettuce in bowl; sprinkle with croutons, anchovies and cheese. To prepare Soft Egg Dressing, boil egg 1 minute. Break egg into a bowl, scraping it out of shell; add remaining dressing ingredients and whisk until smooth. To serve, pour dressing over salad, toss and serve immediately. Makes 4 servings.

Variation: You may also arrange whole inner leaves on 4 individual salad plates. Toss torn lettuce, anchovies, cheese, croutons and dressing in a bowl; spoon atop leaves on plates.

Stuffed Tomato Salad

12 very small firm tomatoes
About 6 tablespoons small-curd cottage
    cheese or ricotta cheese
1 tablespoon half and half
2 oz. smoked or smoked spiced ham,
    finely chopped
1 (1-inch) length cucumber, peeled, fine-
    ly chopped
2 teaspoons chopped fresh dill
Fresh dill sprigs
8 to 12 small lettuce leaves of your
    choice
1 to 2 tablespoons Herb Vinaigrette, page
    11

Using a serrated knife, cut tops off tomatoes. Set tops aside. With knife tip, carefully cut around inside of each tomato; then scoop out center of each tomato with a small spoon. (Discard centers or reserve for another use.) Turn tomato shells upside down on paper towels to drain. In a bowl, beat cottage or ricotta cheese and half and half until smooth. Stir in ham, cucumber and chopped dill. Carefully spoon into tomatoes and replace tops. Garnish each with a dill sprig. Toss lettuce leaves in vinaigrette and arrange on 4 plates. Put 3 tomatoes on each plate and serve. Makes 4 servings.

Variation: If desired, cut tomatoes as shown in the photograph, leaving a "handle" on each one rather than cutting off tops completely. Carefully scoop out centers and pulp beneath "handle." Lay shells on their sides to drain before stuffing them.

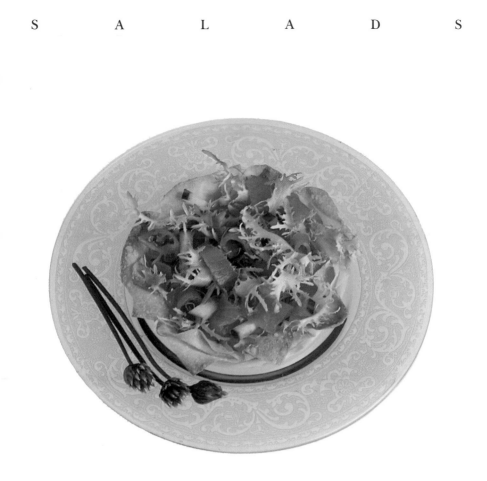

Smoked Salmon Nests

1 or 2 sheets filo pastry, thawed if frozen
2 tablespoons butter, melted
2 to 3 cups bite-size pieces of chicory
1 (1-inch) length cucumber
4 oz. smoked salmon
3 to 4 tablespoons Lemon Vinaigrette,
    page 10

Preheat oven to 400F (205C). Cut each pastry sheet into 3-1/2-inch squares (you need 12 squares). Brush both sides of each square with butter. Arrange 3 squares, overlapping, in each of 4 deep muffin cups. Gently press pastry against pans, then bake 10 minutes or until crisp and golden. Carefully remove from pans; let cool. Put chicory in a bowl. Cut cucumber into sticks; cut salmon into thin strips. Add cucumber and salmon to chicory. Toss with vinaigrette. Pile into cooled pastry shells and serve. Makes 4 servings.

Leeks à la Grecque

1 lb. young, slender leeks
3 tablespoons olive oil
1 medium onion, finely chopped
1 tablespoon water
3 tomatoes, peeled, seeded, chopped
1 garlic clove, crushed
2/3 cup dry white wine
12 coriander seeds
1 bay leaf
Pinch of red (cayenne) pepper
Salt and black pepper to taste
2 teaspoons chopped fresh thyme
1 tablespoon olive oil
2 or 3 pitted ripe olives, chopped
Fresh thyme sprig, if desired

Trim leeks and rinse thoroughly, washing out all dirt. Cut into 2- to 3-inch lengths. Blanch in boiling water 2 minutes; drain and set aside. Heat 3 tablespoons oil in a large saucepan. Add onion and 1 tablespoon water, reduce heat and cook gently 8 minutes. Add tomatoes, garlic, wine, coriander seeds, bay leaf and red pepper. Cook about 15 minutes or until tomatoes are quite soft and have released their juice. Add blanched leeks and cook, uncovered, 10 to 15 minutes or until tender; if mixture begins to get too dry, add a little water. Season with salt and black pepper. Discard bay leaf. Let leek mixture cool. Transfer to a serving dish, sprinkle with chopped thyme and refrigerate until serving time. To serve, drizzle with 1 tablespoon oil and sprinkle with olives; garnish with thyme sprig, if desired. Makes 4 servings.

Marinated Mushrooms

2 tablespoons olive oil
1 shallot, finely chopped
4 oz. fresh shiitake mushrooms, stems removed, or any large mushrooms, sliced
6 tablespoons dry white wine
4 oz. fresh button mushrooms, stems trimmed
4 oz. fresh oyster mushrooms, stems trimmed
1 teaspoon pickled pink peppercorns, drained
1 teaspoon pickled green peppercorns, drained
3 tablespoons walnut oil
1/2 teaspoon Dijon-style mustard
Salt to taste
1 teaspoon chopped fresh oregano
Fresh oregano sprig, if desired

Heat olive oil in a skillet, add shallot and cook 2 minutes. Add shiitake mushrooms and sauté 2 to 3 minutes; pour in wine and simmer 2 minutes. Remove from heat, pour into a bowl and let cool. Then pour through a strainer, reserving cooking liquid. Slice button mushrooms. Halve any large oyster mushrooms. Mix shiitake, button and oyster mushrooms with pink and green peppercorns. Whisk walnut oil and mustard into reserved cooking liquid. Season with salt. Pour over mushroom mixture and toss to mix. Sprinkle with chopped oregano and let marinate up to 1 hour before serving. Garnish with oregano sprig, if desired. Makes 4 servings.

Smoked Fish Platter

2 smoked trout fillets
2 peppered smoked mackerel or smoked
    whitefish fillets
3 slices firm-textured white bread,
    toasted
2 tablespoons butter, room temperature
1 teaspoon lemon juice
1 (3-1/2-oz.) can smoked oysters, drained
Small lettuce leaves of your choice
Lemon slices and fresh dill sprigs
Horseradish Sauce, see below

Horseradish Sauce:
6 tablespoons plain yogurt
4 teaspoons prepared horseradish
2 teaspoons lemon juice
4 teaspoons chopped parsley
Black pepper to taste

Skin trout fillets and cut into small pieces. Skin mackerel or whitefish fillets; break into small pieces. Using a small fancy cutter, cut out rounds from toast (you need about 12 rounds total). Beat together butter and lemon juice; spread a little on toast rounds. Place a smoked oyster on each round. Arrange fish and oyster-topped toast on 4 plates. Garnish with lettuce leaves, lemon slices and dill sprigs. To prepare Horseradish Sauce, thoroughly blend all ingredients. Spoon into a serving dish and offer to accompany salads. Makes 4 servings.

Stilton & Walnut Salad

2 medium heads Belgian endive
2 heads Little Gem lettuce, shredded, or
    about 4 cups shredded inner romaine
    lettuce leaves
1 large ripe pear
2 oz. Blue Stilton cheese, grated (about
    1/2 cup)
Walnut Dressing, see below
Walnut halves

Walnut Dressing:
1/2 cup walnut pieces
1/4 cup sunflower oil
2 tablespoons lemon juice
2 tablespoons apple juice
Salt and black pepper to taste

Chop endive and place in a bowl with shredded lettuce. Peel, quarter and core pear; then cut each quarter into thin slices. Add pear and cheese to endive and lettuce; toss to mix. To prepare Walnut Dressing, place all dressing ingredients in a blender and process until smooth. Pour dressing over salad and toss together. Divide salad among 4 plates and garnish with walnut halves. Makes 4 servings.

Gazpacho Jellied Salad

1 lb. ripe tomatoes, peeled, chopped
1 small onion, chopped
1 garlic clove, crushed
1/2 teaspoon celery salt
1 teaspoon tomato paste
1 teaspoon white wine vinegar
1 (1/4-oz.) envelope unflavored gelatin
1/4 cup cold water
Salt and black pepper to taste
1 (3-inch) length cucumber, peeled,
    diced
1/4 mild white or yellow onion, finely
    diced
1/2 green bell pepper, seeded, diced
2 celery stalks, diced
Alfalfa or other sprouts

Place tomatoes, chopped onion, garlic, celery salt, tomato paste and vinegar in a medium saucepan. Bring to a boil; reduce heat and simmer until tomatoes are soft and have released their juice. Press through a strainer into a 4-cup measuring cup. Set aside. In a small saucepan, sprinkle gelatin over water and let stand about 5 minutes or until spongy. Then stir over low heat until gelatin is dissolved. Let cool, then stir into cooled tomato mixture. You need 2-1/2 cups; add water if necessary. Season with salt and pepper. Pour into 4 individual 3/4-cup ring molds and refrigerate until set. To unmold, dip each mold up to rim in a bowl of hot water for a few seconds, then invert onto a plate and lift off mold. Arrange cucumber, onion, bell pepper and celery evenly around salads; place sprouts in center of each salad. Makes 4 servings.

Italian Seafood Salad

2 lbs. live mussels, scrubbed, de-bearded
1 lb. small live hard-shell clams,
  scrubbed
1 tablespoon extra-virgin olive oil
3 small whole squid, cleaned and prepared as directed for Indonesian Seafood Starter, page 31
6 oz. shelled, deveined cooked shrimp
Dressing, see below
Flat-leaf parsley sprigs
Lemon wedges, if desired

Dressing:
5 tablespoons extra-virgin olive oil
2 tablespoons lemon juice
1 tablespoon chopped parsley
1 garlic clove, finely chopped
1 tablespoon capers, drained
Salt and black pepper to taste

In a large saucepan, combine mussels and 1 cup water and bring to a boil. Reduce heat, cover and simmer 5 to 10 minutes or until shells open. Remove from heat. Discard any mussels that remain closed. When mussels are cool enough to handle, remove them from shells. Set aside. Then cook clams and remove from shells as directed for mussels. Heat oil in a heavy skillet, add squid rings and tentacles and sauté 2 to 3 minutes or until opaque. Turn into a bowl and add mussels, clams and shrimp. To prepare Dressing, stir together all ingredients. Pour over seafood mixture, cover and refrigerate 2 hours, stirring occasionally. Garnish salad with parsley and, if desired, lemon wedges before serving. Makes 4 servings.

Caponata

2 medium eggplants
Salt
1/2 cup olive oil
1 small onion, chopped
4 celery stalks, chopped
1 (about 1-lb.) can tomatoes
2 to 3 tablespoons red wine vinegar
1 tablespoon sugar
1 tablespoon capers, drained
12 pitted green olives, chopped
1 tablespoon pine nuts, lightly toasted
Salt and black pepper to taste
1 tablespoon chopped parsley

Cut eggplants into small cubes and place in a colander. Sprinkle with salt and set aside to drain 1 hour. Meanwhile, heat 2 tablespoons oil in a skillet over medium heat, add onion and cook 5 minutes or until softened. Add celery and cook 3 minutes longer. Drain tomatoes, reserving juice; chop tomatoes. Stir chopped tomatoes and their juice into skillet; simmer, uncovered, 5 minutes. Stir in vinegar and sugar and simmer 15 minutes longer. Set aside. Rinse eggplant cubes and pat dry on paper towels. Heat remaining 6 tablespoons oil in a very large skillet, add eggplant and cook until tender and golden, turning often. Stir in tomato mixture, capers, olives and pine nuts; season with salt and pepper. Continue to simmer 2 to 3 minutes longer. Turn into a bowl; let cool. (For best flavor, refrigerate 24 hours to allow flavors to mingle.) Sprinkle with parsley before serving. Makes 6 servings.

Variation: For a more substantial dish, garnish the Caponata with flaked tuna.

Celery Root & Mussels

2 tablespoons lemon juice
1-1/2 lbs. celery root
2 lbs. live mussels, scrubbed, de-bearded
1 cup dry white wine
Remoulade Sauce, see below

Remoulade Sauce:
5 tablespoons mayonnaise, preferably
   homemade, page 12
2 teaspoons chopped sweet or dill
   pickles
1 teaspoon chopped capers
1 teaspoon chopped parsley
1 teaspoon anchovy paste

Half-fill a large saucepan with water; add lemon juice. Bring to a boil. Meanwhile, scrub and peel celery root, then cut into thin slices; immediately drop slices into boiling water-lemon juice mixture. Reduce heat, cover and simmer 4 to 5 minutes or just until tender. Drain; cut slices into thin strips, place in a bowl and let cool. Place mussels in a large saucepan, add wine, cover and cook over high heat until mussels open. Remove from heat. Discard any mussels that remain closed. Drain mussels, reserving cooking liquid. Reserve a few mussels in their shells for garnish; remove remainder from shells and add to celery root. To prepare Remoulade Sauce, place all sauce ingredients in a bowl with 2 to 3 tablespoons of the reserved mussel cooking liquid. Mix well to make a sauce with the consistency of whipping cream. Stir sauce into celery root and mussels. Spoon into a serving dish or individual dishes. Garnish with reserved mussels in the shell. Makes 4 servings.

Kipper Salad

3 large undyed kippers
2 tablespoons light olive oil
1/4 cup lemon juice
1 teaspoon sugar
1 onion, sliced, separated into rings
1 bay leaf
About 1 cup alfalfa or other sprouts
1 lemon, thinly sliced

Bone and skin kippers. Slice flesh and place in a glass dish. Pour oil and lemon juice over fish; top with sugar, onion and bay leaf. Mix well. Cover and refrigerate 24 hours, stirring occasionally. Discard bay leaf. Drain kipper mixture and divide among 4 plates. Garnish each serving with sprouts and lemon slices. Makes 4 servings.

Indonesian Seafood Starter

8 oz. small whole squid
12 oz. uncooked shrimp in the shell
1 tablespoon sunflower oil
1 small onion, finely chopped
1 garlic clove, crushed
3 tomatoes, peeled, chopped
1 tablespoon dark soy sauce
1 teaspoon ground ginger
1 small fresh green chili, seeded, finely
   chopped
1 tablespoon red wine vinegar
1/2 red bell pepper, seeded, cut into thin
   strips
1/2 green bell pepper, seeded, cut into
   thin strips

To clean squid, hold body in 1 hand and base of tentacles just above eyes in other hand. Pull gently to separate body and tentacles. Pull out and discard transparent "pen" from body; pull out and discard viscera and ink sac. Rinse body cavity. Pull off and discard any membrane covering body. Cut body crosswise into thin rings. Cut off tentacles just above eyes; discard eyes. Squeeze beak from base of tentacles; discard. Rinse tentacles. Set squid aside. Shell shrimp, leaving tail shells intact; set aside. Heat oil in a medium saucepan, add onion and cook until soft. Add garlic, tomatoes, soy sauce, ginger, chili and vinegar; cook 5 minutes. Stir squid rings and tentacles and shelled shrimp into sauce; cook, uncovered, 5 minutes or until squid is opaque and shrimp turn pink. Let seafood cool in sauce, then divide between 4 dishes and garnish with bell pepper strips. Makes 4 servings.

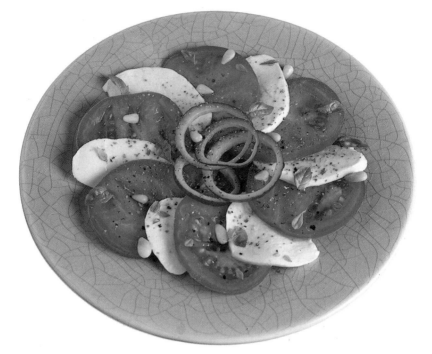

Tomato & Mozzarella Salad

2 large beefsteak tomatoes, sliced
6 oz. mozzarella cheese, sliced
1 small red onion, sliced, separated into
**   rings**
Salt and black pepper to taste
1/4 cup extra-virgin olive oil
1 tablespoon fresh basil leaves
1 tablespoon pine nuts

Arrange tomato slices and cheese slices on 4 plates. Top with onion rings. Season with salt and pepper, then drizzle with oil. Sprinkle with basil and pine nuts and serve. Makes 4 servings.

Spinach & Bacon Salad

6 to 8 cups young spinach leaves,
  washed well, trimmed
2 oz. fresh button mushrooms, stems
  trimmed, sliced
3 thick slices bread, crusts removed
1/4 cup sunflower oil
1 garlic clove, crushed
6 oz. sliced bacon, chopped
2 tablespoons white wine vinegar
Freshly ground black pepper to taste

Tear spinach into bite-size pieces. Place spinach and mushrooms in a salad bowl. Cut bread into small squares. Heat oil in a skillet, add bread squares and garlic and cook until bread is crisp and golden, turning frequently. Remove with a slotted spoon and drain on paper towels. Wipe out skillet with paper towels. Add bacon and cook about 5 minutes or until crisp and browned. Pour bacon and its drippings over spinach mixture. Add vinegar to skillet with a few grinds of pepper; bring to a boil, then immediately pour over salad and toss. Sprinkle salad with croutons, spoon onto plates and serve at once. Makes 6 servings.

Avocado Crab Louis

Seafood Sauce, see below
8 oz. plain white crabmeat, flaked
2 medium avocados
Lemon juice
Lemon slices
Fresh chervil sprigs
Brown bread and butter (in pinwheels, if
    desired)

Seafood Sauce:
1/4 cup mayonnaise, preferably home-
    made, page 12
1 tablespoon ketchup
1/2 teaspoon Worcestershire sauce
1/4 cup half and half
2 teaspoons lemon juice
Dash of dry sherry
Pinch of red (cayenne) pepper

To prepare Seafood Sauce, place all sauce ingredients in a bowl and blend well. Fold crabmeat into sauce. Pit, peel and slice avocados, then brush with lemon juice to prevent discoloration. Arrange avocado slices on 4 plates. Divide crabmeat mixture evenly among plates; garnish with lemon slices and chervil sprigs. Serve with brown bread and butter. Makes 4 servings.

Smoked Chicken Exotica

**8 to 10 oz. smoked chicken or turkey
   breast**
**1 carambola (starfruit), sliced, any seeds
   removed**
1 papaya, peeled, seeded, sliced
2 fresh figs, quartered
1 mango, peeled, flesh sliced off pit
1/4 cup sunflower oil
1 tablespoon sherry vinegar
Pinch of apple pie spice
1 tablespoon chopped preserved ginger

Slice chicken or turkey. Arrange meat
slices, carambola slices, papaya slices
and figs on 4 plates. Dice half the mango and arrange on plates. Place remaining mango in a blender with oil, vinegar
and spice. Process until smooth. Drizzle
over salads (or spoon in center of
salads). Garnish with ginger. Makes 4
servings.

Chicken Livers Tièdes

1 medium (about 6-oz.) thin-skinned
   potato, peeled, cut into 1/4-inch-thick
   julienne strips
About 2 cups fresh broccoli flowerets
2 slender zucchini, sliced
8 oz. chicken livers
1/4 cup virgin olive oil
Salt and black pepper to taste
2 tablespoons sherry vinegar
2 shallots, thinly sliced

Cook potato in boiling water 5 to 7 minutes or until tender. Drain well and set aside. In another saucepan, cook broccoli in boiling water 3 minutes; then add zucchini and cook 1 minute longer. Drain broccoli and zucchini in a colander. Set aside. Rinse chicken livers; trim off membranes. Pat livers dry on paper towels. Heat oil in a skillet; add livers and sprinkle with salt and pepper. Cook 5 minutes, stirring and turning livers so they cook evenly. They should still be soft and pink in center. Lift from skillet with a slotted spoon. Divide drained vegetables among 4 plates; slice livers and scatter over vegetables. Stir vinegar into drippings in skillet, warm quickly and pour over salads. Sprinkle with shallots and serve. Makes 4 first-course servings.

Sole with Caper Dressing

Lemon Marinade, see below
2 (about 8-oz.) sole fillets, skinned
6 tablespoons dry white wine
2 heads Belgian endive, chopped
1 bunch watercress, trimmed
2 teaspoons capers

Lemon Marinade:
1/4 cup light olive oil
Peel (colored part only) of 1 lemon, cut
   into very thin shreds
2 tablespoons lemon juice
1 tablespoon chopped parsley
1 shallot, finely chopped
Salt and black pepper to taste

To prepare Lemon Marinade, stir all marinade ingredients together in a bowl. Set aside. Cut sole fillets in half lengthwise, then cut crosswise into thin strips. Place in a skillet with wine; bring to a simmer, cover and simmer 2 minutes or until opaque. Lift sole from skillet (reserve cooking liquid) and put into marinade. Let stand 10 minutes. Arrange endive and watercress on 4 plates. Remove fish from marinade (reserve marinade) and divide among plates. Boil cooking liquid rapidly to reduce liquid to 1/4 cup; add capers and reserved marinade and heat just until warm. Quickly pour over salads and serve at once. Makes 4 first-course servings.

—— Lobster & Asparagus ——

1 medium (about 1-1/2-lb.) lobster
8 oz. fresh asparagus, tough stalk ends
    removed, spears cut into 2-inch
    pieces
About 2 cups shredded tender green cab-
    bage
Tarragon Dressing, see below
Fresh tarragon sprigs

Tarragon Dressing:
3 tablespoons virgin olive oil
1 tablespoon tarragon vinegar
2 teaspoons chopped fresh tarragon
Salt and black pepper to taste

Remove lobster claws. Crack open large claws and remove meat, trying to keep it in chunks. Using tip of a sharp knife, split lobster in half from head to tail. Starting at tail, remove tail meat; discard brown, feathery gills. Remove liver; reserve for another recipe, if desired. Remove and reserve dark coral if present. Extract meat from body. Slice tail meat. Set all lobster meat aside. In a vegetable steamer over boiling water, steam asparagus 7 minutes or until almost tender. Add cabbage and steam 2 minutes longer. Arrange lobster meat and steamed vegetables on 4 plates. To prepare Tarragon Dressing, stir together all dressing ingredients. Drizzle dressing over salads. Garnish with reserved lobster coral and tarragon sprigs. Serve at once, while vegetables are warm. Makes 4 first-course servings.

Goat Cheese Salad

1 head radicchio
About 1 cup sliced celery
Walnut Dressing, see below
4 slices whole-grain bread, toasted
2 (4-oz.) wheels goat cheese
2 celery stalks, chopped
About 1/4 cup chopped walnuts
Celery leaves

Walnut Dressing:
3 tablespoons walnut oil
1 tablespoon red wine vinegar
1 small garlic clove, crushed
Salt and black pepper to taste

Separate radicchio leaves and place in a bowl along with sliced celery. Prepare Walnut Dressing by stirring together all dressing ingredients; pour over radicchio and celery and toss to mix, then arrange on 4 plates. Cut out 4 rounds from centers of toast slices. Cut each cheese in half horizontally; trim off any crust from ends. Place a cheese slice on each toast round; then arrange on a baking sheet and broil 3 to 4 minutes or until cheese is just starting to turn golden. Transfer to plates, sprinkle with chopped celery and walnuts, garnish with celery leaves and serve at once. Makes 4 first-course servings.

Shrimp with Snow Peas

12 large uncooked shrimp in the shell
8 oz. snow peas, ends and strings
   removed
3 tablespoons virgin olive oil
1 tablespoon finely shredded fresh
   ginger
Juice and grated peel of 1 lime
1 tablespoon soy sauce

Shell shrimp, leaving tail shells intact. Remove veins. Set shrimp aside. Cook snow peas in boiling water 1 minute. Drain and arrange on 4 plates. Heat oil in a large skillet, add shrimp and ginger and cook gently 5 minutes or until shrimp turn pink, turning shrimp over halfway through cooking. Add lime juice, lime peel and soy sauce. Cook 1 minute longer. Arrange shrimp atop snow peas; pour hot pan juices over shrimp and serve. Makes 4 first-course servings.

Calf's Liver Balsamico

2 large (8-oz.) slices calf's liver
A few escarole leaves
A few radicchio or lollo rosso leaves
2 to 3 cups mâche (lamb's lettuce)
1/4 cup extra-virgin olive oil
1 tablespoon shredded fresh sage
2 tablespoons balsamic vinegar
Salt and black pepper to taste
1 tablespoon pine nuts

Rinse liver; trim off any membranes and large veins. Pat liver dry and cut into thin strips. Set aside. Tear escarole, radicchio or lollo rosso and mâche into smaller pieces. Arrange on 4 plates. Heat oil in a skillet. Add liver and sage and cook 2 to 3 minutes or until liver is browned on outside but still pink inside, stirring constantly. Remove liver from skillet with a slotted spoon and divide among plates. Pour vinegar into drippings in skillet; heat to warm through. Season with salt and pepper, then spoon over greens and liver on plates. Sprinkle with pine nuts and serve. Makes 4 first-course servings.

Duck with Kumquats

2 whole duck or chicken breasts,
 skinned, boned, split
About 2/3 cup dry white wine
Pinch of ground ginger
8 coriander seeds, crushed
Salt and black pepper to taste
12 fresh kumquats, sliced
3 tablespoons hazelnut oil
2 teaspoons lemon juice
3 to 4 cups young spinach leaves,
 washed well, trimmed
1/2 pomegranate, peel and pith removed,
 seeds separated

Place duck or chicken in a large skillet, add wine, sprinkle with ginger and coriander and season with salt and pepper. Bring to a boil; reduce heat, cover and simmer about 15 minutes or until meat is tender, adding a little more wine if necessary. Add kumquats and simmer 1 minute longer. Lift meat and kumquats from skillet and set aside. Boil cooking liquid rapidly to reduce it to 1/4 cup; stir in oil and lemon juice and warm through. Slice meat; arrange meat, kumquat slices and spinach attractively on 4 dinner plates. Pour warm dressing over salads, sprinkle with pomegranate seeds and serve. Makes 4 main-course servings.

Lamb with Spaghetti Squash

Red Pepper Dressing, see below
1 (about 1-1/2-lb.) spaghetti squash
About 1/2 cup frozen peas
1-1/4 to 1-1/2 lbs. thinly sliced rare roast lamb
Regular-strength beef or chicken broth
Salt and black pepper to taste
Fresh rosemary sprigs

Red Pepper Dressing:
2 small red bell peppers, roasted (see page 110), skins and seeds removed
2 teaspoons sherry vinegar
6 tablespoons virgin olive oil
Salt and black pepper to taste

To prepare dressing, combine bell peppers, vinegar and oil in a blender; process until smooth. Season with salt and pepper and set aside. Cut squash in half lengthwise and remove seeds. Place squash, cut side down, in a large saucepan and add enough water to come halfway up sides of pan. Bring to a boil; reduce heat, cover and simmer 15 to 20 minutes or until squash is tender. Remove from pan; scoop flesh from shells with a fork and place in a colander to drain. Also cook peas in a little boiling water 2 to 3 minutes; drain. Place lamb slices in a large skillet, add a little broth and heat just until meat is warmed through. Season drained squash with salt and pepper; divide among 6 dinner plates. Arrange lamb on plates. Spoon some of Red Pepper Dressing over salads; offer remaining dressing separately. Garnish each plate with a spoonful of peas and a few rosemary sprigs. Makes 6 main-course servings.

Peppery Chicken Salad

1/4 head chicory
2 to 3 cups torn lollo rosso or red leaf
  lettuce leaves
2 to 3 cups mâche (lamb's lettuce)
3 or 4 tomatoes, peeled, seeded, cut into
  thin wedges
2 whole chicken breasts, skinned, boned,
  split
1-1/4 cups dry white wine
Salt and black pepper to taste
1-1/2 teaspoons pickled green peppercorns, drained
5 tablespoons half and half

Tear any large leaves of chicory into smaller pieces. Divide chicory, lollo rosso or lettuce and mâche among 4 dinner plates. Arrange tomatoes atop greens. Place chicken in a large skillet, add wine and season with salt and pepper. Bring to a boil; reduce heat, cover and simmer about 15 minutes or until chicken is tender. Lift from skillet (reserve cooking liquid); place on a board and let cool slightly, then slice. Add peppercorns to cooking liquid and boil rapidly to reduce to 5 tablespoons. Stir in half and half and heat to warm through. Arrange chicken atop salads, pour on dressing and serve immediately. (You may also pass dressing at the table.) Makes 4 main-course servings.

Hot Sausage Salad

About 2 cups finely shredded red cabbage
About 2 cups finely shredded green cabbage
1 medium tart apple
1 teaspoon lemon juice
1 (about 1-lb.) ring-shaped pork sausage
Mustard Mayonnaise, see below
Chopped parsley and parsley sprigs

Mustard Mayonnaise:
3 tablespoons mayonnaise, preferably
homemade, page 12
3 tablespoons soft cream cheese
1 tablespoon whole-grain mustard
3 tablespoons apple juice
Salt and black pepper to taste

Combine red and green cabbage in a
bowl. Core and grate apple, toss with
lemon juice and add to cabbage. Set
aside. Cook sausage according to package directions. Meanwhile, prepare
Mustard Mayonnaise by stirring
together all ingredients. Stir Mustard
Mayonnaise into cabbage mixture.
Spoon onto individual serving plates.
Slice cooked sausage and arrange
alongside cabbage mixture. Garnish
with parsley and serve. Makes about 6
first-course servings.

Oriental Chicken Salad

8 radishes, cut into roses or fans
2 whole chicken breasts, cooked,
   skinned, boned
About 3 cups fresh bean sprouts
4 oz. fresh button mushrooms, stems
   trimmed, sliced
1 yellow bell pepper, seeded, diced
3 green onions, chopped
2 carrots, cut into thin julienne strips
1 recipe Oriental Dressing, page 15
1 tablespoon sesame seeds, toasted

Place radishes in a bowl of ice water to make them open. Meanwhile, shred chicken and place in a bowl with bean sprouts, mushrooms, bell pepper, green onions and carrots. Stir together. Pour dressing over salad; toss to mix. Transfer salad to a serving dish; sprinkle with sesame seeds and garnish with radishes. Makes 4 servings.

Thai Seafood Salad

8 oz. monkfish fillets, skinned if necessary, cubed
4 scallops
1 (8-oz.) salmon steak, skinned, cubed, any large bones removed
8 large uncooked shrimp, shelled, deveined
1 (2-inch) piece fresh ginger, peeled, slivered
2 bulbs (white stalk bases) of lemon grass, peeled, chopped
Juice of 1 lime
4 teaspoons light soy sauce
2 teaspoons chopped fresh mint
1 tablespoon chopped fresh cilantro (coriander)
1 garlic clove, crushed
Rice Salad, see below

Rice Salad:
3-1/2 tablespoons wild rice
1(1-inch) piece fresh ginger, halved
3-1/2 tablespoons long-grain white rice
2 green onions (green part only), shredded
6 coriander seeds, crushed
1 tablespoon light sesame oil

Put monkfish, scallops, salmon and shrimp in a single layer on a rimmed plate. Scatter ginger and lemon grass over seafood. Place plate on a steaming rack above 1 to 1-1/2 inches of boiling water in a wok or deep pan. Cover and steam 5 to 6 minutes or until fish and scallops are opaque throughout and shrimp turn pink. In a dish, stir together lime juice, soy sauce, mint, cilantro and garlic. Add cooked seafood along with 2 tablespoons of cooking juices; gently turn to coat with marinade. Let marinate at least 1 hour. To prepare Rice Salad, place wild rice and ginger in a saucepan of simmering water, cover and cook 30 minutes. Add white rice; cook 20 minutes longer or until all rice is tender. While rice is cooking, put green onion shreds in a bowl of ice water to make them curl. Drain cooked rice and discard ginger, then stir in coriander seeds and sesame oil. To serve, arrange seafood on 4 plates, spooning marinade over it. Divide Rice Salad among plates; garnish with shreds of green onion. Makes 4 servings.

Salade Niçoise

4 oz. thin green beans, ends trimmed
6 small tomatoes, quartered
1/2 cucumber, peeled, diced
1 red bell pepper, seeded, sliced
6 green onions, chopped
1 (6-1/2- to 7-oz.) can tuna, drained,
    flaked
1/2 cup pitted ripe olives
Vinaigrette Dressing, see below
1 tablespoon chopped parsley
3 hard-cooked eggs, quartered
1 (2-oz.) can flat anchovy fillets, drained
Fresh basil leaves

Vinaigrette Dressing:
1/4 cup extra-virgin olive oil
1 tablespoon red wine vinegar
1 tablespoon lemon juice
1/4 teaspoon Dijon-style mustard
Salt and black pepper to taste

Cook beans in boiling water about 5 minutes or just until tender. Drain; rinse with cold water and drain again, then cut into 1-1/2-inch lengths. Put into a bowl with tomatoes, cucumber, bell pepper, green onions, tuna and olives; toss together. To prepare Vinaigrette Dressing, stir together all dressing ingredients. Add dressing to salad along with parsley; toss. Arrange eggs on salad. Cut anchovy fillets in half lengthwise and arrange in a crisscross pattern atop salad. Garnish with basil before serving. Makes 4 servings.

Coronation Chicken

1 (4-lb.) broiler-fryer chicken, poached
   or boiled, cooled
Curry Mayonnaise, see below
Paprika
1 carrot, sliced, cut into flowers
1 celery stalk, cut into thin strips

Curry Mayonnaise:
1/4 cup mayonnaise, preferably homemade, page 12
2 tablespoons lemon juice
2 tablespoons half and half
5 tablespoons plain yogurt
1 teaspoon tomato paste
1 teaspoon curry paste (or use curry
   powder to taste)
2 tablespoons mango chutney

Remove and discard skin and bones
from chicken. Cut meat into neat, bite-
size pieces and place on a platter. To
prepare Curry Mayonnaise, place all
ingredients in a blender and process
until smooth. Pour Curry Mayonnaise
over chicken. Dust with paprika. Garnish with carrot flowers and celery
strips and serve. Makes 6 servings.

Chinese Cabbage Salad

1 small (1-lb.) head Chinese cabbage,
    chopped
6 green onions, shredded
About 3/4 cup whole-kernel corn, thawed
    if frozen
4 oz. snow peas, ends and strings re-
    moved
1 fresh red chili, seeded if desired, thin-
    ly sliced
3 eggs
A few drops of light soy sauce
1 tablespoon sunflower oil
3 tablespoons sesame seeds, toasted
1-1/2 recipes Sesame Dressing, page 15
Red chili flower

Combine cabbage, green onions and corn in a bowl. Cook snow peas in boiling water 30 seconds; drain well, cut in half and add to cabbage mixture with sliced chili. Transfer to a serving dish. Make omelets: Break 1 egg into a bowl and beat in a few drops of soy sauce. Heat 1 teaspoon oil in a small skillet or omelet pan and pour in egg. Tilt pan so egg coats it evenly; cook until egg is set. Turn out onto a plate and sprinkle with 1 tablespoon sesame seeds; roll up jelly-roll style and let cool. Repeat with remaining 2 eggs, 2 teaspoons oil and 2 tablespoons sesame seeds to make 2 more omelets. Pour Sesame Dressing over salad and toss to mix. Cut omelets into 1-inch slices and arrange atop salad before serving. Makes 4 servings.

Malaysian Salad

Peanut Sauce, see below
About 3 cups shredded green cabbage
4 oz. thin green beans, ends trimmed, cut
  into 1-inch lengths
1/2 small cauliflower, broken into small
  flowerets
About 2 cups fresh bean sprouts
1/2 cucumber
Fresh cilantro (coriander) leaves

Peanut Sauce:
1/3 cup unsweetened grated coconut
2/3 cup boiling water
3 tablespoons peanut butter
2 teaspoons soy sauce
Juice of 1/2 lime
1/4 teaspoon chili powder

To prepare Peanut Sauce, place coconut in a bowl and pour boiling water over it. Let soak 15 minutes. Pour mixture through cheesecloth into another bowl, pressing to extract liquid (discard coconut). Add remaining sauce ingredients; mix well. Set aside. Fill a large saucepan with water; bring to a boil. Add cabbage, beans and cauliflower; boil 2 to 3 minutes. Drain vegetables thoroughly; arrange on a platter or 4 individual plates. Scatter bean sprouts over vegetables. Score sides of cucumber deeply with a fork or cut strips of peel from sides with a vegetable peeler. Slice cucumber; arrange around salad. Spoon Peanut Dressing onto center of salad or serve separately. Garnish salad with cilantro. Makes 4 servings.

—— Stuffed Egg Taramasalata Salad ——

6 large hard-cooked eggs
1 (4-oz.) jar taramasalata
1 tablespoon black or red lumpfish
   caviar
6 small tomatoes, finely diced
1/2 cucumber, peeled if desired, finely
   diced
1 small green bell pepper, seeded, finely
   diced
1 small avocado, pitted, peeled, diced
1/2 recipe Lemon Vinaigrette, page 10
Fresh dill sprigs

Halve eggs crosswise. Remove yolks and put in a bowl. Cut a thin slice off end of each egg white so halves will sit flat. Beat together egg yolks and taramasalata; spoon into egg whites. Garnish each with a little caviar. In a bowl, mix tomatoes, cucumber, bell pepper and avocado with Lemon Vinaigrette. Spoon onto a serving plate or 4 individual plates; arrange stuffed eggs on top. Garnish with dill sprigs. Makes 4 servings.

Pasta Pesto Salad

8 oz. dried orzo (rice-shaped pasta)
8 oz. cherry tomatoes, quartered
Pesto Dressing, see below
About 1/4 cup pine nuts, lightly toasted
Fresh basil sprigs

Pesto Dressing:
About 1 cup lightly packed fresh basil
    leaves
2 garlic cloves, peeled
About 1/4 cup pine nuts
3 tablespoons virgin olive oil
1/4 cup freshly grated Parmesan cheese
    (3/4 oz.)
3 tablespoons half and half

Following package directions, cook pasta in boiling salted water just until tender but still firm. Drain, rinse with cold water and drain again. Place in a bowl and add tomatoes. To prepare Pesto Dressing, combine basil leaves, garlic, pine nuts and oil in a blender and process until smooth. Turn into a bowl and beat in cheese and half and half. Stir dressing into pasta mixture, then transfer to a serving dish and sprinkle with toasted pine nuts. Garnish with basil sprigs. Makes 4 side-dish servings.

Italian Salami Salad

1 (about 15-oz.) can navy beans or can-
    nellini (white kidney beans), drained
1 fennel bulb, trimmed, thinly sliced
1 small green bell pepper, seeded, diced
4 oz. sliced Italian salami
Garlic Dressing, see below
Shredded fresh basil
Tomato wedges
Ripe olives

Garlic Dressing:
3 tablespoons extra-virgin olive oil
1 tablespoon white wine vinegar
1 garlic clove, crushed
Salt and black pepper to taste

Combine beans, fennel and bell pepper
in a bowl. Cut salami slices into quarters
and add to salad. To prepare Garlic
Dressing, stir together all dressing ingredients. Pour dressing over salad;
toss to mix. Spoon into a serving dish
and garnish with basil, tomato wedges
and olives. Makes 4 servings.

Stroganoff Salad

Lettuce leaves of your choice
12 oz. cold rare roast beef, cut into thin strips
8 oz. fresh button mushrooms, stems trimmed, sliced
6 green onions, chopped or shredded
1 red bell pepper, seeded, thinly sliced
Sour Cream Dressing, see below
Shredded lettuce of your choice

Sour Cream Dressing:
2/3 cup dairy sour cream
1 tablespoon prepared horseradish
2 teaspoons lemon juice
Salt and black pepper to taste

Line a serving dish with lettuce leaves. Combine beef, mushrooms, green onions and bell pepper in a bowl. To prepare Sour Cream Dressing, stir together all dressing ingredients. Stir dressing into salad. Spoon salad into lettuce-lined dish. Garnish with shredded lettuce and serve. Makes 4 servings.

Spanish Paella Salad

2 tablespoons olive oil
1 medium onion, chopped
1 garlic clove, crushed
1-3/4 cups arborio (medium-grain) rice
Pinch of saffron threads
3-1/2 cups hot regular-strength chicken
    broth
8 oz. tomatoes, peeled, seeded, chopped
About 3/4 cup frozen peas, thawed
2 whole chicken breasts, cooked,
    skinned, boned, diced
6 oz. chorizo sausage, casings removed,
    sliced, browned, drained
1 red or green bell pepper, seeded, sliced
3 tablespoons extra-virgin olive oil
1 tablespoon lemon juice
1/2 teaspoon paprika
Salt and black pepper to taste
Pimento-stuffed green olives

Heat 2 tablespoons oil in a large sauce-pan. Add onion and garlic; cook over medium-low heat until soft. Add rice and cook 2 minutes. Stir in saffron and hot broth, cover and simmer about 20 minutes or until rice is tender and all liquid has been absorbed. Remove from heat; transfer to a bowl to cool. Fluff up cooked rice with a fork and add tomatoes, peas, chicken, sausage and bell pepper. Stir together 3 tablespoons oil, lemon juice, paprika, salt and pepper; pour over salad and mix well. Garnish with olives and serve. Makes 4 servings.

Eggs Tonnato

Tonnato Sauce, see below
6 large hard-cooked eggs
Pimento strips
1 (2-oz.) can flat anchovy fillets, drained
Fresh dill sprigs

Tonnato Sauce:
1 recipe Mayonnaise, page 12
1 small (3-1/2-oz.) can tuna, drained
1 tablespoon lemon juice
1 tablespoon half and half or plain
   yogurt
1 teaspoon capers, drained, chopped

To prepare Tonnato Sauce, place Mayonnaise in a blender along with tuna, lemon juice and half and half or yogurt. Process until smooth; stir in capers. Halve eggs lengthwise and place 3 halves on each of 4 plates. Spoon sauce over eggs; decorate with pimento strips. To garnish salad, halve anchovy fillets; roll up each half and place between eggs. Top with dill sprigs and serve. Makes 4 servings.

Pasta & Shrimp Salad

8 oz. dried small pasta shells (use part or
all spinach shells, if desired)
12 oz. shelled, deveined cooked shrimp
4 oz. smoked salmon, cut into thin strips
Herb Dressing, see below
Fresh tarragon sprigs

Herb Dressing:
4-1/2 tablespoons virgin olive oil
1-1/2 tablespoons lemon juice
1-1/2 tablespoons tomato juice
1-1/2 tablespoons chopped parsley
1-1/2 tablespoons chopped fresh tarragon
Salt and black pepper to taste

Following package directions, cook
pasta in boiling salted water just until
tender but still firm. Drain, rinse with
cold water and drain again. Place in a
bowl with shrimp and salmon. To prepare Herb Dressing, stir all dressing ingredients together. Pour over salad,
toss to mix and transfer to a serving
dish. Garnish with tarragon sprigs.
Makes 4 main-dish servings.

Barbecued Steak Salad

Marinade, see below
4 (6-oz.) tenderloin steaks
Avocado Dressing, see below
Greens of your choice
Cherry tomatoes

Marinade:
1/4 cup sunflower oil
2 tablespoons red wine vinegar
1 tablespoon tomato paste
2 teaspoons Worcestershire sauce
1 teaspoon Dijon-style mustard
1 garlic clove, crushed
1/2 teaspoon paprika
Salt and black pepper to taste

Avocado Dressing:
1 small ripe avocado
Juice of 1 lemon
1/4 cup virgin olive oil
1 garlic clove, crushed
1/4 cup half and half
Salt and black pepper to taste

In a glass dish, stir together all Marinade ingredients. Add steaks, turning them to coat with Marinade; let marinate 1 hour. To prepare Avocado Dressing, halve and pit avocado; scoop flesh into a blender and add lemon juice, oil, garlic and half and half. Process until smooth; season with salt and pepper. (This dressing should be used within 2 hours of being made.) Arrange greens on 1 side of each of 4 plates. Grill or broil steaks, turning as needed, until browned on outside, rare inside. Place cooked steaks on a board and quickly slice them, cutting straight down. Arrange sliced steak on plates alongside greens. Garnish with tomatoes and accompany with Avocado Dressing. Makes 4 servings.

Lake Trout Salad

2 large lake trout, cleaned
Salt and black pepper to taste
Sunflower oil
4 carrots
2 zucchini
1 (6-inch) length cucumber
About 1 cup alfalfa sprouts
1/2 recipe Vinaigrette Dressing, page 10
1 tablespoon chopped fresh tarragon
1 head Bibb lettuce
Nasturtium blossoms or watercress
    sprigs

Sprinkle trout with salt and pepper; brush with a little oil. Arrange on a broiler pan; broil, turning once, until opaque throughout. Let cool. Remove skin and bones; break flesh into neat pieces. Set aside. Peel carrots; then use a vegetable peeler to cut them into thin, broad ribbons (discard centers of carrots). Place carrot strips in a bowl. Cut zucchini diagonally into thin slices. Cook slices in boiling water 1 minute. Drain; add to carrots. Score sides of cucumber deeply with a fork or cut strips of peel from sides with a vegetable peeler. Cut cucumber in half lengthwise, then slice. Add cucumber and alfalfa sprouts to carrots and zucchini in bowl. Stir together Vinaigrette Dressing and tarragon; pour over vegetables and toss. Add trout and toss gently. Line 4 plates with lettuce; divide salad among plates. Garnish with nasturtium blossoms or watercress. Makes 4 servings.

Herringsalat

Marinade, see below
4 fresh herrings, cleaned, scaled, boned
2 large dill pickles, diced
8 oz. potatoes, cooked, peeled, diced
3 or 4 green onions, chopped
6 tablespoons plain yogurt
2 tablespoons mayonnaise, preferably
   homemade, page 12
3 medium beets, cooked, peeled, sliced
Snipped chives
Whole chives

Marinade:
1/2 cup cider vinegar
1/2 cup water
2 tablespoons sugar
1 small onion, chopped
1 bay leaf
Generous pinch of black pepper
Generous pinch of ground allspice

To prepare Marinade, combine all Marinade ingredients in a saucepan and bring to a boil. Reduce heat and simmer 1 minute, then remove from heat and let cool. Meanwhile, cut fish into 2-inch pieces and place in a glass dish. Pour Marinade over fish, cover and refrigerate at least 6 hours or (preferably) overnight. Then drain fish and place in a bowl with pickles, potatoes and green onions. Stir together yogurt and mayonnaise; stir into salad. Arrange beets around edge of a serving dish; spoon herring salad in center. Sprinkle with snipped chives; garnish with whole chives. Makes 4 servings.

Smoked Mackerel Salad

1 lb. small thin-skinned potatoes
1 tablespoon olive oil
4 smoked mackerel or smoked whitefish
  fillets
1/2 cucumber, peeled
Mustard Dressing, see below
Parsley sprigs

Mustard Dressing:
2 tablespoons sunflower oil
1 tablespoon whole-grain mustard
1 tablespoon lemon juice

Scrub potatoes, but do not peel. Cook in boiling water until tender; drain. When potatoes are cool enough to handle, peel them; then cut into quarters or thick slices. Place in a bowl; toss with oil. Remove skin from fish fillets. Break flesh into pieces; add to potatoes. Cut cucumber in half crosswise. Dice 1 half and add to salad. Using an apple corer, remove center from remaining cucumber piece; slice cucumber crosswise and set aside. To prepare Mustard Dressing, stir together all dressing ingredients. Stir dressing into salad, then pile onto a serving dish. Garnish salad with cucumber slices and parsley sprigs, then serve. Makes 4 servings.

Dressed Crab

1 small (1-lb.) cooked crab in the shell
1 teaspoon lemon juice
Mayonnaise, preferably homemade, page 12
About 1 cup fresh bread crumbs
Salt and black pepper to taste
1 hard-cooked egg
1 tablespoon chopped parsley
Shredded lettuce of your choice

Hold crab firmly and twist off claws. Pull off upper shell. Turn crab on its back; pull off apron. Discard feathery gills (dead man's fingers), small bile sac lying in top of upper shell and any green matter. Using a teaspoon, scrape all brown meat inside shell into a bowl. Discard membrane attached on either side. Wash and dry upper shell; set aside. Snap legs in half by bending them backwards at joint. Using a hammer, crack shells on legs but do not shatter them; scrape white meat into a separate bowl, using a skewer to get into crevices. Discard any bits of shell. Crack larger claws and remove meat. Cut remaining body section in half and pick out white meat from the honeycomb structure with a skewer. To dress crab, mix brown meat with lemon juice, 1 tablespoon mayonnaise and bread crumbs. Season with salt and pepper, then spoon mixture into center of reserved shell. Using a small spoon, place white meat at both ends of shell. Rub egg yolk through a sieve; chop white. Cover brown meat with egg yolk; sprinkle a line of egg white on either side of this, then a line of parsley. Line a plate with lettuce; place crab on lettuce. Serve with mayonnaise. Makes 1 serving.

Chef's Salad

1/2 head iceberg lettuce
1/2 head Bibb lettuce
4 celery stalks, sliced
1/2 bunch radishes, trimmed, sliced
6 oz. cold cooked chicken
4 oz. cold cooked ham
4 oz. Swiss cheese
Blue Cheese Dressing, see below

Blue Cheese Dressing:
3 tablespoons plain yogurt
3 tablespoons mayonnaise, preferably
    homemade, page 12
2 oz. Danish Blue or Roquefort cheese,
    crumbled (about 1/2 cup)
1 teaspoon lemon juice

Shred iceberg lettuce. Tear Bibb lettuce leaves into smaller pieces. In a
salad bowl, combine lettuces, celery and
radishes. Cut chicken, ham and cheese
into strips; add to salad. To prepare
Blue Cheese Dressing, combine all
dressing ingredients in a blender and
process until smooth. Spoon dressing
over salad; toss to mix. Makes 4 servings.

German Sausage Salad

2 small (7-oz.) fully cooked German
   sausages, such as bierwurst or Bava-
   rian ham sausage
1/2 head Bibb or iceberg lettuce,
   shredded
1 red bell pepper, seeded, diced
1 green bell pepper, seeded, diced
1 large head Belgian endive, sliced
1/2 cucumber, diced
1 recipe Vinaigrette Dressing, page 10
1 teaspoon poppy seeds

Remove casings from sausages; dice
sausages. Put lettuce in bottom of a
glass salad bowl; scatter half the diced
sausage over it. Top evenly with red
and green bell peppers, then sprinkle
on remaining diced sausage. Top with
endive and cucumber; pour Vinaigrette Dressing over salad. Sprinkle
with poppy seeds. Makes about 3 servings.

Marinated Beef Salad

Teriyaki Marinade, see below
1 lb. top round, sirloin or flank steak
1/2 head Chinese cabbage, shredded
1 large carrot
2 green onions or 3 shallots, thinly sliced
1 small tomato

Teriyaki Marinade:
6 tablespoons dry sherry
3 tablespoons soy sauce
1 tablespoon red wine vinegar
2 tablespoons honey
1 garlic clove, crushed
1 teaspoon ground ginger

To prepare Teriyaki Marinade, stir together all marinade ingredients in a dish. Add steak to marinade and turn to coat both sides. Cover and refrigerate overnight, turning once. Preheat broiler. Drain meat, place on a rack in a broiler pan and broil, turning as needed, until well browned outside but still rare inside. Remove from broiler and let cool. Pour any cooking juices into a bowl or measuring cup; refrigerate, then remove fat. Place meat on a board; slice thinly, cutting across the grain. Arrange cabbage on a platter. Arrange meat atop cabbage. Drizzle with reserved cooking juices. Peel carrots; then use a vegetable peeler to cut them into long, thin ribbons (discard centers of carrots). Place carrot strips around edge of platter. Scatter green onions or shallots over meat. Cut peel and some flesh from tomato in a continuous spiral and arrange atop salad to resemble a rose. Makes 4 servings.

Salmagundi

6 oz. thin green beans, ends trimmed, cut into 2-inch lengths
1 head lettuce, such as Bibb or iceberg, shredded
2 hard-cooked eggs, chopped
2 tablespoons chopped parsley
1 (2-oz.) can flat anchovy fillets, drained, chopped
1/2 cucumber, diced
1 tablespoon snipped chives
6 green onions, chopped
3 small tomatoes, seeded, chopped
8 oz. cold cooked chicken, diced
4 oz. cold cooked ham, diced
8 oz. thin-skinned potatoes, cooked, peeled if desired, sliced
1/2 (1-lb.) jar sweet-and-sour red cabbage, drained
1 recipe Vinaigrette Dressing, page 10
1 tablespoon capers, drained
Borage or nasturtium blossoms, if desired

Cook beans in boiling water about 5 minutes or just until tender. Drain, rinse with cold water and drain again. Set aside. Line a platter with lettuce. Toss eggs, parsley and anchovies together. Mix cucumber and chives together; mix green onions and tomatoes together. Arrange these 3 groups of ingredients on lettuce-lined platter along with beans, chicken, ham, potatoes and cabbage. Drizzle with Vinaigrette Dressing. Garnish with capers and blossoms, if desired. Makes 4 servings.

Saffron Rice Ring

2 tablespoons butter
4 cardamom pods
3 whole cloves
1 (2-inch) piece cinnamon stick
1 cup plus 2 tablespoons basmati or
   other long-grain white rice
2-1/2 cups hot regular-strength chicken
   broth
Generous pinch of saffron threads
2 tablespoons hot water
About 3/4 cup frozen tiny peas
3 tablespoons half and half
Salt and black pepper to taste
8 oz. shelled, deveined cooked shrimp
1/2 cucumber, diced
1/4 cup plain yogurt
2 teaspoons chopped fresh mint
Pinch of red (cayenne) pepper
Fresh mint sprigs

Melt butter in a large saucepan. Add cardamom, cloves and cinnamon stick; cook 1 minute. Stir in rice and cook 1 minute. Gradually add hot broth, keeping it simmering as it is added. Cover and simmer 15 to 20 minutes. Put saffron in a cup and pour in hot water; mix well, then stir into rice along with peas. Cook 2 minutes longer. Remove from heat. Remove cardamom, cloves and cinnamon stick; stir in half and half. Season rice mixture with salt and black pepper, then spoon it into a 5-cup ring mold, patting it down with back of a spoon. Let cool completely, then refrigerate 30 minutes before serving. Turn rice ring out onto a plate. Combine shrimp, cucumber, yogurt, chopped mint and red pepper; spoon into center of rice ring. Garnish with mint sprigs. Makes 4 main-course or 6 side-dish servings.

Tonno con Fagioli

1 (about 15-oz.) can cannellini (white kidney beans), drained
1 (about 14-oz.) can flageolets, drained
1/2 red onion, sliced
Salt and black pepper to taste
2 (6-1/2- to 7-oz.) cans tuna, drained
2 tablespoons chopped parsley
5 tablespoons extra-virgin olive oil
1 tablespoon red wine vinegar
Ripe olives
Lemon slices
Flat-leaf parsley sprigs

In a bowl, combine cannellini, flageolets and onion. Season with salt and pepper. Add tuna, breaking it into large flakes with a fork; stir in chopped parsley. Stir together oil and vinegar; season with salt and pepper. Add to salad, tossing to mix well. Transfer to a serving dish and garnish with olives, lemon slices and parsley sprigs. Makes 4 main-course or 6 first-course servings.

Mediterranean Lentils

1 cup brown or green lentils
8 oz. tomatoes, peeled, seeded, diced
3 celery stalks, sliced
4 oz. fresh button mushrooms, stems
    trimmed, sliced
Spicy Lemon Dressing, see below
Celery leaves and lemon slices

Spicy Lemon Dressing:
5 tablespoons virgin olive oil
1 tablespoon lemon juice
1 garlic clove, crushed
1 tablespoon chopped parsley
1/2 teaspoon ground cumin
Salt and black pepper to taste

Rinse and sort lentils; then place in a saucepan and add water to cover. Bring to a boil; reduce heat, cover and simmer 30 minutes or until tender. Drain and place in a bowl with tomatoes, celery and mushrooms. To prepare Spicy Lemon Dressing, stir together all dressing ingredients; pour over salad and stir together. Garnish with celery leaves and lemon slices before serving. Makes 6 side-dish servings.

Bulgur Medley

3 young, slender leeks
2 tablespoons sunflower oil
2 shallots, chopped
1 garlic clove, crushed
1-1/4 cups bulgur (cracked wheat), such as Ala brand
2 cups hot vegetable stock (or use 2 vegetable bouillon cubes dissolved in 2 cups boiling water)
2 carrots, diced
3 celery stalks, sliced
2 zucchini, diced
Tomato Dressing, see below
Salt and black pepper to taste
Fresh cilantro (coriander) leaves

Tomato Dressing:
8 oz. tomatoes, peeled, seeded, finely chopped
3 tablespoons virgin olive oil
1 tablespoon wine vinegar
1 teaspoon tomato paste
1 garlic clove, crushed
1/2 teaspoon paprika
Pinch of sugar

Trim leeks and rinse thoroughly, washing out all dirt; then thinly slice and set aside. Heat oil in a saucepan over medium heat. Add shallots and garlic and cook 2 to 3 minutes. Add bulgur and stir around pan 1 minute. Gradually pour in hot stock and simmer 5 minutes. Add leeks, carrots and celery and cook 5 minutes; then stir in zucchini and cook 2 minutes longer. Remove from heat; let cool. To prepare Tomato Dressing, stir all dressing ingredients together. Stir dressing into bulgur mixture; season with salt and pepper. Garnish with cilantro before serving. Makes 6 to 8 side-dish servings.

Sprouted Bean Salad

About 1/4 cup adzuki beans
About 1/4 cup mung beans
About 1/4 cup green lentils
1 red onion
Honey & Mustard Dressing, see below

Honey & Mustard Dressing:
1/4 cup mayonnaise, preferably home-
    made, page 12
2 tablespoons sunflower oil
1 teaspoon honey
1 tablespoon mild prepared mustard
1 tablespoon lemon juice
Salt and black pepper to taste

Put adzuki beans, mung beans and lentils in 3 separate bowls. Cover with
water and let soak overnight; then
drain each and put in a wide-mouth jar.
Cover jars with cheesecloth; secure
cloth with rubber bands. Set jars in a
warm, dark place 4 to 6 days or until
beans and lentils have sprouted; twice a
day, fill jars with water and drain
through cloth to rinse beans and lentils.
Remove sprouts from jars, rinse again,
drain and store in refrigerator up to 4
days. To serve, cut onion in half
lengthwise, then thinly slice crosswise.
Mix onion and sprouts in a serving dish.
Prepare Honey & Mustard Dressing by
beating together all dressing ingredients until honey is evenly
blended. Pour dressing over salad, toss
and serve. Makes 6 side-dish servings.

Lima Bean Salad

1 cup dried large lima beans, soaked
   overnight, drained (or use about 2-1/2
   cups cooked, drained large lima beans
   or butter beans)
Salt to taste
6 oz. sliced bacon
Tomato Dressing, see below
2 tablespoons snipped chives

Tomato Dressing:
1 large ripe tomato, peeled, seeded,
   chopped
1 teaspoon tomato paste
3 tablespoons extra-virgin olive oil
2 teaspoons lemon juice
Salt and black pepper to taste

If using dried beans, rinse beans. Place in a saucepan and add water to cover; bring to a boil, then reduce heat, cover and simmer about 2 hours or until tender. Add salt during last 5 minutes of cooking. (If using cooked beans, simply pour into a saucepan, add a little water and heat through.) While beans are cooking, cook bacon slices in a skillet until crisp on both sides. Remove from skillet, drain on paper towels and break into small pieces. Set aside. To prepare Tomato Dressing, process all dressing ingredients in a blender until blended. Drain beans and place in a serving dish; pour dressing over beans and let cool. Mix in bacon and sprinkle with chives before serving. Makes 4 to 6 side-dish servings.

Jade Salad

1 cup plus 2 tablespoons long-grain
  white rice
8 oz. frozen chopped spinach (about 3/4
  of a 10-oz. pkg.), thawed
2 tablespoons chopped parsley
6 to 8 green onions, trimmed
1/2 recipe Vinaigrette Dressing, page 10
Salt and black pepper to taste
Green onion brush

Following package directions, cook rice
in boiling salted water until tender.
Drain, rinse with cold water and drain
again. While rice is cooking, squeeze as
much water out of spinach as possible;
then place spinach in a bowl and add
parsley. Reserve 2 green onions; finely
chop remaining onions and add to
spinach. Add warm cooked rice to spinach mixture; stir in Vinaigrette Dressing. Season with salt and pepper. Let
salad cool completely, then refrigerate
before serving. Makes 6 first-course or
side-dish servings.

Curried Rice Salad

1 cup plus 2 tablespoons long-grain
    brown rice
1/2 cup moist-pack dried apricots,
    chopped
3 tablespoons sunflower oil
About 1/2 cup cashews
1 medium onion, chopped
1 teaspoon cumin seeds
1 tablespoon curry powder
6 tablespoons orange juice
6 tablespoons raisins
Salt and black pepper to taste
Fresh cilantro (coriander) sprigs (or
    chopped leaves)

Following package directions, cook rice in boiling salted water until tender. Meanwhile, place apricots in a bowl and add boiling water to cover. Let soak 10 to 15 minutes; then drain. Also heat oil in a skillet, add cashews and cook until golden. Remove from skillet with a slotted spoon and drain on paper towels. Add onion to oil in skillet and cook over medium heat 3 to 4 minutes. Stir in cumin seeds and curry powder and cook 2 minutes. Pour in orange juice; simmer 1 minute. Remove from heat. When rice is done, drain, rinse with cold water, drain again and put in a bowl. Add warm orange juice mixture and mix well; stir in drained apricots, cashews and raisins. Season with salt and pepper. Let salad stand at least 2 hours before serving to allow flavors to mingle. Garnish with cilantro before serving. Makes 6 side-dish servings.

Mexican Bean Salad

1 (about 15-oz.) can red kidney beans,
   drained
1 to 1-1/4 cups whole-kernel corn,
   thawed if frozen
1 green bell pepper, seeded, chopped
3 or 4 green onions, chopped
2 tablespoons chopped fresh cilantro
   (coriander)
Garlic-Lime Dressing, see below
1/2 head iceberg lettuce, if desired,
   shredded
Lime slices
Fresh cilantro (coriander) sprigs

Garlic-Lime Dressing:
1/4 cup virgin olive oil
Juice of 1/2 lime
1 garlic clove, crushed
Salt and black pepper to taste

In a bowl, combine beans, corn, bell pepper, green onions and cilantro. Prepare Garlic-Lime Dressing by stirring together all dressing ingredients; pour over salad and toss together. If desired, line a serving dish with shredded lettuce. Spoon salad into dish; garnish with lime slices and cilantro sprigs. Makes 4 to 6 side-dish servings.

Tabbouleh

1 cup bulgur (cracked wheat)
1/4 cup lemon juice
1/4 cup virgin olive oil
Salt and black pepper to taste
1 tablespoon finely chopped mild white
  or yellow onion
6 green onions, finely chopped
1 small bunch flat-leaf parsley, trimmed,
  chopped
About 3/4 cup chopped fresh mint
1 head romaine lettuce
Cherry tomatoes
Flat-leaf parsley sprigs

Place bulgur in a bowl and add warm water to cover. Let soak 30 minutes. Squeeze out excess water; put bulgur in a bowl. Add lemon juice, oil, salt and pepper, white or yellow onion, green onions, chopped parsley and mint. Mix to combine well, then refrigerate at least 1 hour before serving. To serve, arrange lettuce leaves around edge of a platter; spoon tabbouleh in center of platter and garnish with tomatoes and parsley sprigs. Makes 6 side-dish servings.

Spiced Garbanzo Bean Salad

3 tablespoons olive oil
1 small onion, finely chopped
1 fresh green chili, seeded, finely
  chopped
1 garlic clove, finely chopped
2 teaspoons ground coriander
1 teaspoon ground cumin
1 teaspoon ground turmeric
2 tablespoons plain yogurt
2 (about 15-oz.) cans garbanzo beans,
  drained
Salt and black pepper to taste
2 tablespoons chopped fresh cilantro
  (coriander)

Heat oil in a small skillet. Add onion, chili and garlic; cook 2 to 3 minutes. Stir in ground coriander, cumin and turmeric; cook 1 minute longer. Turn into a large bowl and stir in yogurt. Add beans to spice mixture and mix well. Season with salt and pepper. Cover and let stand at least 2 hours before serving. Garnish with cilantro before serving. Makes 6 side-dish servings.

Japanese Vinegared Rice

**4 oz. snow peas, ends and strings re-
moved**
**3/4 cup plus 2 tablespoons long-grain
white rice**
2 tablespoons rice vinegar
1 tablespoon light sesame oil
1 teaspoon dark sesame oil
4 teaspoons tamari (Japanese soy sauce)
4 green onions, chopped

Cook snow peas in boiling water 30
seconds; drain, rinse with cold water
and pat dry on paper towels. Arrange
around edge of a serving dish; cover
and refrigerate. Following package directions, cook rice in boiling salted
water until tender. Drain, rinse with
cold water, drain again and place in a
bowl. Stir together vinegar, light and
dark sesame oils, tamari and green
onions; then stir into rice. Spoon rice
mixture into serving dish. Makes 4 to 6
side-dish servings.

Variation: Wrap small portions of the
prepared dressed rice in blanched spinach or grape leaves (or rinsed canned
grape leaves); cut these rolls in half and
stand them on end to resemble sushi.

Hummus Salad

1 (about 15-oz.) can garbanzo beans,
   drained
1/4 cup virgin olive oil
3 tablespoons tahini (sesame-seed paste)
2 garlic cloves, peeled
Juice of 1 lemon
Salt and black pepper to taste
Paprika
Ripe olives and fresh cilantro (coriander)
   leaves
Crudités, such as carrot sticks or baby
   carrots, celery sticks, and radishes

In a blender or food processor, combine beans, 3 tablespoons oil, tahini, garlic and lemon juice. Process until smooth; season with salt and pepper. Spoon into a serving bowl or 4 individual dishes. Drizzle remaining 1 tablespoon oil over top, dust with paprika and garnish with olives and cilantro. Serve with a selection of crudités. Makes 4 first-course servings.

Three-Bean Salad

6 oz. thin green beans, ends trimmed, cut into 1-1/2-inch lengths
8 oz. shelled fresh lima or fava beans (or use 1-3/4 cups frozen baby green lima beans)
1-1/2 cups canned red kidney beans, drained, rinsed
Shallot Dressing, see below
Shallots, sliced, separated into rings

Shallot Dressing:
6 tablespoons virgin olive oil
1-1/2 to 2 tablespoons red wine vinegar
2 small shallots, finely chopped
Salt and black pepper to taste

Cook green beans in boiling water about 5 minutes or just until tender. Drain. In another saucepan, cook fresh lima or fava beans in boiling water 20 to 25 minutes or until tender; drain. While beans are still warm, slip off skins. (Or cook frozen baby limas according to package directions; drain.) In a bowl, combine green beans, lima or fava beans and kidney beans. To prepare Shallot Dressing, stir together all dressing ingredients. Pour dressing over salad. Transfer to a serving dish; garnish with shallot rings. Cover and refrigerate until ready to serve. Makes 4 to 6 side-dish servings.

Thousand Island Seafood Salad

1-1/2 lbs. firm white-fleshed fish fillets,
   such as cod, lemon sole, halibut or
   sea bass
Juice of 1 lemon
Salt and black pepper to taste
Thousand Island Dressing, see below
2 kiwifruit
2 tamarillos
1 small mango

Thousand Island Dressing:
1 recipe Mayonnaise, page 12
1 teaspoon tomato paste
1 tablespoon lemon juice
6 pimento-stuffed green olives, chopped
2 green onions, finely chopped
1 tablespoon chopped parsley
1 hard-cooked egg, chopped
1/2 teaspoon paprika
1/2 teaspoon sugar

Preheat oven to 375F (190C). Remove any skin from fish; place fish in a baking dish and sprinkle with lemon juice, salt and pepper. Cover and bake until fish is just opaque throughout, allowing 8 to 10 minutes for each inch the fillets are thick. Let fish cool, then cut into cubes. Spoon a little of the cooking juices over fish to keep it moist. To prepare Thousand Island Dressing, stir together all dressing ingredients. Set aside. Peel and slice kiwifruit and tamarillos. Peel mango and cut flesh from pit in strips. Arrange fish and fruit on dinner plates. Spoon dressing over all, then serve. Makes 4 main-course servings.

TIP: To peel tamarillos, plunge into boiling water for about 30 seconds, then drain; slip off skins.

Gingered Pork & Lychees

2 tablespoons light sesame oil
1 lb. pork tenderloin, cut into thin strips
1 garlic clove, crushed
1 tablespoon chopped fresh ginger
3 oz. snow peas, ends and strings removed, cut into thin strips
1 (about 15-oz.) can lychees, drained
Sweet & Sour Dressing, see below
1/2 head Chinese cabbage, shredded
Chili flowers

Sweet & Sour Dressing:
2 tablespoons light sesame oil
4 teaspoons rice vinegar
2 teaspoons dark soy sauce
1 teaspoon honey
1 teaspoon tomato paste

Heat oil in a large skillet or wok. Add pork, garlic and ginger; cook until meat is lightly browned. Add snow peas and cook 30 seconds. Remove from heat. Using a slotted spoon, transfer pork and snow peas to a bowl; add lychees. To prepare Sweet & Sour Dressing, stir together all dressing ingredients. Pour over pork mixture; let cool. To serve, spread cabbage on a platter or 4 individual plates. Spoon pork mixture over cabbage; garnish with chili flowers. Makes 3 or 4 main-course servings.

Chicken & Grape Salad

4 oz. red or purple grapes
4 oz. green grapes
1 lb. cold cooked, boned chicken, diced
3 celery stalks, chopped
Tarragon Dressing, see below
1/2 head lettuce of your choice, if de-
    sired, finely shredded
Nasturtium petals
Fresh tarragon sprigs

Tarragon Dressing:
1/4 cup virgin olive oil
4 teaspoons tarragon vinegar
1/4 cup dairy sour cream
Salt and black pepper to taste

Halve grapes (reserve a few whole grapes for garnish, if desired). If you are not using seedless grapes, remove seeds. In a bowl, combine grapes, chicken and celery. To prepare Tarragon Dressing, stir together all dressing ingredients. Pour dressing over salad; toss together. Line 4 dinner plates with lettuce, if desired. Spoon chicken salad onto plates. Garnish with any reserved whole grapes, nasturtium petals or tarragon sprigs. Makes 4 main-course servings.

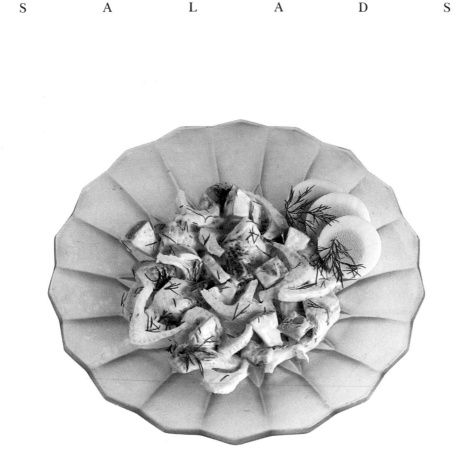

Rollmops & Apple Salad

2 green-skinned apples, such as Granny
   Smith
1-1/2 tablespoons lemon juice
8 "rollmop" herrings
1 fennel bulb, trimmed, thinly sliced
Sour Cream & Dill Dressing, see below
2 hard-cooked eggs, sliced
Fresh dill sprigs

Sour Cream & Dill Dressing:
2/3 cup dairy sour cream
2 tablespoons plain yogurt
2 teaspoons prepared horseradish
1 tablespoon chopped fresh dill
Salt and black pepper to taste

Core and dice apples; place in a bowl, add lemon juice and toss to mix. Cut herring into bite-size pieces and add to apples along with fennel. To prepare Sour Cream & Dill Dressing, stir together all dressing ingredients. Stir dressing into salad. Transfer to a serving dish and garnish with egg slices and dill sprigs. Makes 4 main-course or 6 first-course servings.

Cheese & Fruit Platter

2 green-skinned apples, such as Granny
    Smith
Juice of 1/2 lemon
4 oz. smoked Cheddar or Swiss cheese,
    cubed
1 (8-oz.) wedge Brie cheese, sliced cross-
    wise; or 1 whole (7- to 8-oz.) Camem-
    bert cheese, cut into thin wedges
2 to 4 celery stalks, sliced
6 oz. red, green or purple grapes
Celery leaves or alfalfa or other sprouts
1/3 cup mayonnaise, preferably home-
    made, page 12
1/2 teaspoon finely grated lemon peel
2 teaspoons lemon juice

Core and slice apples; brush with
lemon juice. Arrange apple slices and
cheese on 4 dinner plates; attractively
arrange celery slices and grapes alongside. Garnish with celery leaves or
sprouts. Stir together mayonnaise,
lemon peel and lemon juice; spoon into
a bowl and offer alongside salad, or
spoon into 4 small bowls or cups and
provide each diner with a cup of dressing. Makes 4 light main-course servings.

Variation: Use other cheese and fruits
of your choice, such as Gouda, Jarl-
sberg or blue cheese and pears, plums
or nectarines.

Turkey & Cranberry Salad

1 lb. uncooked turkey breast slices
Juice of 1 lime
1/2 cup dry vermouth
2 teaspoons honey
1/2 teaspoon dried leaf oregano
Salt and black pepper to taste
2 tablespoons virgin olive oil
1 small onion, chopped
1 cup fresh or frozen cranberries
Slivered peel of 1/2 orange
Orange slices
Watercress sprigs

Cut turkey slices into thin strips. In a bowl, mix lime juice, vermouth, honey, oregano, salt and pepper. Stir in turkey and let marinate 2 hours. Lift turkey from marinade; drain (reserve marinade). Heat oil in a skillet, add turkey and onion and cook 5 minutes. Pour reserved marinade into skillet; stir in cranberries and orange peel. Cook gently until cranberries begin to split. Transfer to a dish and let cool. To serve, stir salad, then place in a serving dish. Garnish with orange slices and watercress sprigs. Makes 3 or 4 main-course servings.

Nectarines with Prosciutto

Greens of your choice
2 nectarines
4 oz. thinly sliced prosciutto
3 tablespoons virgin olive oil
5 teaspoons sunflower oil
1 tablespoon raspberry vinegar
Fresh raspberries

Line 4 plates with greens. Slice nectarines. Halve each slice of prosciutto. Wrap each nectarine slice in prosciutto; arrange atop greens. Whisk together olive oil, sunflower oil and vinegar; drizzle over salad. Garnish with raspberries and serve. Makes 4 first-course servings.

Avocado & Strawberries

Honey Lemon Dressing, see below
1 (1-pt.) basket strawberries
2 small avocados
Fresh mint leaves or strawberry leaves

Honey Lemon Dressing:
2 tablespoons sunflower oil
2 teaspoons honey
2 tablespoons lemon juice
1/4 teaspoon paprika
Salt and black pepper to taste

To prepare Honey Lemon Dressing, stir together all dressing ingredients. Set aside. Hull strawberries; cut into slices or halves. Pit, peel and dice avocados. Arrange avocados and berries on 4 serving plates; drizzle with dressing. Garnish with mint or strawberry leaves and serve. Makes 4 first-course servings.

Shrimp with Grapefruit

About 2 cups young, small spinach
  leaves, washed well, trimmed
1 bunch watercress, trimmed
2 ruby-red grapefruit
6 oz. shelled, deveined cooked medium
  to large shrimp
Fresh chervil sprigs
Grapefruit-Yogurt Dressing, see below

Grapefruit-Yogurt Dressing:
2 tablespoons plain yogurt
2 tablespoons virgin olive oil
1 teaspoon honey
2 tablespoons grapefruit juice (reserved
  from grapefruit in salad)
Salt and black pepper to taste

Tear large spinach leaves into smaller pieces. Mix watercress with spinach; divide among 4 serving plates. With a sharp knife, cut peel and all white pith from grapefruit. To section each grapefruit, hold it over a bowl to catch juice; cut between segments and lift them free. Arrange grapefruit segments and shrimp over spinach mixture. Garnish salads with chervil sprigs. To prepare Grapefruit-Yogurt Dressing, stir together all dressing ingredients until honey is thoroughly incorporated. Spoon dressing over salad or offer dressing at the table. Makes 4 first-course servings.

Melon & Tomato Salad

1 small honeydew melon or 2 small cantaloupe melons
12 oz. tomatoes, peeled
Mint Dressing, see below
Fresh mint sprigs

Mint Dressing:
2 tablespoons sunflower oil
2 teaspoons sherry vinegar
1 tablespoon chopped fresh mint
Black pepper to taste

Cut melon(s) in half and scoop out seeds. Using a melon baller or a knife, cut flesh into cubes or balls; place in a bowl. (If using cantaloupes, reserve shells to use as serving dishes, if desired.) Quarter and seed tomatoes; cut each quarter crosswise into 4 pieces and add to melon. To prepare Mint Dressing, stir together all dressing ingredients. Pour dressing over salad; toss to mix. Refrigerate. (Also cover and refrigerate melon shells, if used.) Remove salad from refrigerator 30 minutes before serving. Spoon into 4 dishes (or into melon shells), garnish with mint sprigs and serve. Makes 4 first-course servings.

Waldorf Salad

3 red-skinned apples
2 tablespoons lemon juice
5 celery stalks, thinly sliced
About 1/2 cup coarsely chopped walnuts
1/2 teaspoon caraway seeds
1/2 cup mayonnaise, preferably home-
    made, page 12
Walnut halves
Celery leaves

Core and dice apples, then place in a bowl and toss with lemon juice to prevent discoloration. Add sliced celery, chopped walnuts and caraway seeds. Toss to mix, then stir in mayonnaise. Spoon salad into a salad bowl, garnish with walnut halves and celery leaves and serve. Makes 6 side-dish servings.

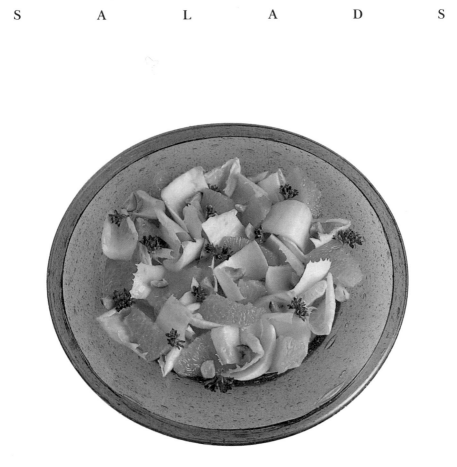

Endive & Orange Salad

1/2 cup hazelnuts
4 medium heads Belgian endive
3 oranges
Hazelnut Dressing, see below
1 tablespoon chopped parsley

Hazelnut Dressing:
3 tablespoons hazelnut oil
3 tablespoons orange juice (reserved
    from oranges in salad)
Pinch of apple pie spice
Salt and black pepper to taste

Preheat oven to 350F (175C). Spread hazelnuts evenly on a rimmed baking sheet; bake 10 to 15 minutes or until pale golden beneath skins. Let cool briefly; then pour onto a dish towel, fold towel to enclose and rub briskly to remove as much of skins as possible. Coarsely chop nuts; set aside. Chop endive and place in a bowl. With a sharp knife, cut peel and white pith from oranges. To section each orange, hold it over a bowl to catch juice; cut between segments and lift them free. Cut each segment in half and add to endive. To prepare Hazelnut Dressing, stir together all dressing ingredients. Pour dressing over salad and toss to mix; transfer salad to a serving bowl. Sprinkle with hazelnuts, garnish with parsley and serve. Makes 4 to 6 side-dish servings.

Avocado & Citrus Salad

1/2 head chicory
2 oranges
1 grapefruit
1 ripe avocado
Citrus Dressing, see below
Fresh mint sprigs

Citrus Dressing:
1 tablespoon sunflower oil
1 tablespoon each orange juice and
    grapefruit juice (reserved from fruit
    in salad)
Juice of 1/2 lime
1 tablespoon chopped fresh mint
Salt and black pepper to taste

Tear chicory leaves into smaller pieces and place in a salad bowl. With a sharp knife, cut peel and all white pith from oranges and grapefruit. Holding fruit over a bowl to catch juice, cut between segments and lift them free. Halve segments, if desired, then arrange atop chicory. Pit, peel and thinly slice avocado; then add to salad. To prepare Citrus Dressing, stir together all dressing ingredients. Spoon dressing over salad, garnish with mint sprigs and serve. Makes 4 side-dish servings.

Persian Carrot Salad

2 large oranges
1 lb. carrots, grated
1/2 cup raisins
1/2 cup blanched almonds, lightly
   toasted
2 tablespoons virgin olive oil
2 tablespoons lime juice
1 teaspoon ground cumin
1/2 teaspoon ground cinnamon
1/2 teaspoon superfine sugar
Lime slices

With a sharp knife, cut peel and all white pith from oranges. To section each orange, hold it over a bowl to catch juice; cut between segments and lift them free. Cut each segment into bite-size pieces; place in another bowl. (Reserve orange juice for another use.) To oranges in bowl, add carrots, raisins and almonds; mix. Stir together oil, lime juice, cumin, cinnamon and sugar; pour over salad and toss to mix. Refrigerate 1 hour. Garnish with lime slices before serving. Makes 6 side-dish servings.

Fruity Coleslaw

12 oz. white or light green cabbage, finely shredded
1 (14-oz.) can pineapple slices or 1 (12-oz.) fresh pineapple, chopped
1-1/2 eating apples
2 teaspoons lemon juice
1/3 cup raisins
1/3 cup salted peanuts
1/2 apple, sliced or pineapple leaves to garnish

Dressing:
1 recipe Mayonnaise, page 12
1 teaspoon clear honey
3 tablespoons pineapple or honey juice
Salt and pepper

Put cabbage into a large bowl. If using canned pineapple, drain well, reserving the juice, and chop the fruit. Add pineapple to cabbage. Core and chop apples, toss in lemon juice and add to salad with raisins and peanuts. To make the dressing, mix all the ingredients in a bowl, using reserved pineapple juice or apple juice, then pour over the salad. Mix well, then turn into a serving dish. Garnish and serve at once. Makes 6 to 8 servings as a side salad.

Apple & Celery Root Salad

1/4 cup lemon juice
1 medium celery root
3 green-skinned apples, such as Granny Smith
2 teaspoons poppy seeds
1/4 cup plain yogurt
3 tablespoons apple juice
Salt and black pepper to taste
Parsley sprigs

Half-fill a large saucepan with water; add 2 tablespoons lemon juice. Bring to a boil. Meanwhile, scrub and peel celery root, then cut into 1/2-inch-thick slices. Immediately drop slices into boiling water-lemon juice mixture. Reduce heat, cover and simmer 7 to 8 minutes or just until tender. Drain and let cool, then dice and set aside. Quarter and core apples. Dice 8 quarters; slice remaining 4 quarters. Place all apples in a bowl, add remaining 2 tablespoons lemon juice and toss together; then remove apple slices and reserve for garnish. Mix celery root with diced apples. Stir together poppy seeds, yogurt and apple juice; season with salt and pepper. Pour over salad; toss to mix. Transfer to a serving dish and garnish with reserved apple slices and parsley sprigs. Makes 6 side-dish servings.

Classic Tomato Salad

1 lb. firm-ripe tomatoes
1 teaspoon sugar
Salt and black pepper to taste
6 tablespoons virgin olive oil
2 tablespoons white wine vinegar
1 tablespoon snipped chives

Thinly slice tomatoes and arrange on a serving plate. Sprinkle with sugar and season with salt and pepper. Stir together oil and vinegar and spoon over salad. Sprinkle with chives, then cover and refrigerate at least 1 hour before serving. Makes 4 servings.

Variation: Sprinkle salad with finely chopped green onion or shredded fresh basil instead of chives.

German Potato Salad

2 lbs. thin-skinned potatoes, scrubbed,
   unpeeled
6 green onions, finely chopped
1/3 cup mayonnaise, preferably homemade, page 12
1/3 cup plain yogurt
Salt and black pepper to taste
Snipped chives

Cook potatoes in boiling salted water until tender. Drain and let cool. Dice cooled potatoes and place in a bowl; add green onions. Stir together mayonnaise and yogurt and fold into salad. Season with salt and pepper. Spoon into a salad bowl; sprinkle with chives before serving. Makes 6 servings.

Beet & Onion Salad

1 lb. beets, cooked, peeled, cut into thin
   julienne strips
2 shallots, finely chopped
1/4 cup Vinaigrette Dressing, page 10
Lettuce leaves of your choice
1/2 small onion, thinly sliced, separated
   into rings
1 tablespoon chopped parsley

In a glass dish, mix beets, shallots and Vinaigrette Dressing. Let marinate 2 hours. Line a serving dish with lettuce leaves; spoon in salad and scatter onions on top. Garnish with parsley and serve. Makes 4 to 6 servings.

Coleslaw

Boiled Dressing, see below
1 lb. green cabbage, shredded
2 medium carrots, coarsely grated
5 celery stalks, sliced
2 tablespoons chopped parsley
Celery leaves, if desired

Boiled Dressing:
2 tablespoons sunflower oil
1 tablespoon all-purpose flour
1 teaspoon dry mustard
1/2 cup water
2 teaspoons white wine vinegar
1 egg, beaten
Salt and black pepper to taste
Pinch of red (cayenne) pepper
Pinch of sugar

To prepare Boiled Dressing, blend oil, flour and mustard in a saucepan. Slowly stir in water, vinegar, egg, salt, black pepper, red pepper and sugar. Cook over very low heat, stirring constantly, until dressing is thickened. Remove from heat; let cool slightly. Meanwhile, place cabbage, carrots, and celery in a bowl; toss to mix. Pour dressing over salad and mix well. Let cool completely. Before serving, sprinkle with parsley and garnish with celery leaves, if desired. Makes 6 to 8 servings.

Greek Salad

1/2 head romaine lettuce, chopped
A few young spinach leaves, washed
   well, shredded
3 tomatoes, cut into wedges
1/2 cucumber, halved lengthwise, sliced
1/2 mild white or yellow onion, thinly
   sliced, separated into rings
1 green bell pepper, seeded, sliced
6 oz. feta cheese, cubed
About 12 kalamata or pitted ripe olives
1 teaspoon chopped fresh oregano or
   marjoram
Lemon Dressing, see below

Lemon Dressing:
1/4 cup extra-virgin olive oil
1 tablespoon lemon juice
Salt and black pepper to taste

Mix lettuce and spinach; place in a
large bowl or individual bowls. Add
tomatoes, cucumber, onion and bell
pepper. Arrange cheese and olives on
top and sprinkle with oregano or marjoram. To prepare Lemon Dressing,
stir together all dressing ingredients.
Spoon dressing over salad and serve.
Makes 4 servings.

Cauliflower Salad

1 cauliflower
1 bunch radishes, trimmed, quartered
2/3 cup plain yogurt
4 teaspoons tahini (sesame-seed paste)
1 teaspoon honey
Salt and black pepper to taste
2 teaspoons toasted sesame seeds

Break cauliflower into small flowerets. Cook in boiling water 2 minutes; drain and let cool. Place in a bowl and mix in radishes. Stir together yogurt, tahini, honey, salt and pepper until smooth. Pour over salad and mix. Turn into a serving dish and sprinkle with sesame seeds. Makes 6 servings.

Whole Wheat Pasta Salad

4 oz. dried whole wheat pasta twists or
  other shapes
6 oz. shelled fresh lima or fava beans (or
  use about 1-1/4 cups frozen baby
  green lima beans)
About 2 cups fresh broccoli flowerets
3 oz. snow peas, ends and strings removed
3 tomatoes, diced
1/2 recipe Garlic Vinaigrette, page 11
1 teaspoon chopped fresh oregano

Following package directions, cook pasta in boiling salted water until tender but still firm. Drain, rinse with cold water and drain again. Set aside to cool. Cook fresh lima or fava beans in boiling water 20 to 25 minutes or until tender; drain. While beans are still warm, slip off skins. (Or cook frozen baby limas according to package directions; drain.) Arrange broccoli flowerets and snow peas in a vegetable steamer; steam over boiling water 3 to 5 minutes or until broccoli is bright green but still crisp. Cut snow peas in half. Put pasta, beans, broccoli, snow peas and tomatoes in a bowl. Add Garlic Vinaigrette and toss together. Transfer to a serving dish and sprinkle with oregano. Makes 4 or 5 servings.

Chinatown Salad

1 (4-oz.) jar miniature corn on the cob, drained
1 (8-oz.) can water chestnuts, drained, sliced
1/2 red bell pepper, seeded, thinly sliced
1 (2-inch) length cucumber
About 3 cups fresh bean sprouts
1 (1/2-inch) piece fresh ginger, peeled, finely shredded
1 recipe Chinese Dressing, page 15
1 head lettuce of your choice
Fresh cilantro (coriander) leaves

In a bowl, combine corn, water chestnuts and bell pepper. Cut cucumber in half lengthwise; cut halves diagonally into strips. Add to corn mixture along with bean sprouts and ginger; toss to mix. Pour Chinese Dressing over salad. Toss to mix, then place in a serving dish lined with lettuce leaves. Garnish with cilantro and serve. Makes 6 servings.

French Potato Salad

1-1/2 lbs. thin-skinned potatoes,
    scrubbed, unpeeled
6 tablespoons virgin olive oil
1-1/2 tablespoons white wine vinegar
Salt and black pepper to taste
3 to 4 tablespoons chopped mixed fresh
    herbs

Cook potatoes in boiling salted water until tender. Drain and let cool briefly; then peel. Leave small potatoes whole; cut larger ones into slices, halves or quarters. Place in a bowl and, while still warm, drizzle with 2 tablespoons oil. Let cool. Stir together remaining 4 tablespoons oil and vinegar; stir into potatoes. Season with salt and pepper. Just before serving, sprinkle salad with herbs; gently fold in. Makes 4 to 6 servings.

Winter Red Salad

1 head oak leaf lettuce or 1 small head
   red leaf lettuce
1 head radicchio
1 red onion, thinly sliced
About 1-1/3 cups shredded red cabbage
About 1 cup diced cooked beets
Walnut Vinaigrette, see below
1/2 pomegranate, peel and pith removed,
   seeds separated

Walnut Vinaigrette:
3 tablespoons walnut oil
1-1/2 tablespoons virgin olive oil
1-1/2 tablespoons red wine vinegar
3/4 teaspoon Dijon-style mustard
Pinch of sugar
Salt and black pepper to taste

Tear large lettuce and radicchio leaves into smaller pieces. Arrange lettuce and radicchio in a bowl. Add onion, cabbage and beets. To prepare Walnut Vinaigrette, stir together all vinaigrette ingredients. Pour vinaigrette over salad and toss. Sprinkle with pomegranate seeds and serve. Makes 4 to 6 servings.

Zucchini Salad

1 lb. zucchini, coarsely grated
Salt
Herb Mayonnaise, see below
Fresh herb sprigs or leaves of your
   choice
Baby zucchini with blossoms attached

Herb Mayonnaise:
2 tablespoons mayonnaise, preferably
   homemade, page 12
1/4 cup plain yogurt
2 teaspoons chopped parsley
2 teaspoons chopped fresh tarragon
2 teaspoons chopped fresh chervil
2 teaspoons snipped chives
Black pepper to taste

Spread grated zucchini on 3 layers of paper towels, sprinkle with salt and let stand 1 hour. Meanwhile, prepare Herb Mayonnaise by stirring together all ingredients in a large bowl. Add zucchini to Herb Mayonnaise in bowl and stir to mix. Spoon into a serving dish, garnish with baby zucchini and serve. Makes 4 servings.

Tricolor Pasta Salad

8 oz. dried tricolor rotelle (corkscrew
   pasta)
1 tablespoon virgin olive oil
4 oz. fresh button mushrooms or wild
   mushrooms, stems trimmed, sliced
1/2 cup pitted green olives, chopped
1 (2-oz.) can flat anchovy fillets, drained,
   cut into thin strips
1 tablespoon chopped fresh oregano
3 tablespoons virgin olive oil
1-1/2 tablespoons balsamic vinegar
Salt and black pepper to taste

Following package directions, cook
pasta in boiling salted water until tender but still firm. Drain, rinse with cold
water and drain again. Set aside. Heat 1
tablespoon oil in a skillet, add mushrooms and cook 2 to 3 minutes. Let
cool; then place in a bowl with cooked
pasta, olives, anchovies and oregano.
Stir together 3 tablespoons oil and vinegar; pour over salad. Toss together;
season with salt and pepper and serve.
Makes 4 to 6 servings.

Sweet Pepper Salad

2 large red bell peppers
2 large yellow bell peppers
6 tablespoons extra-virgin olive oil
2 garlic cloves, peeled
Salt and black pepper to taste
Ripe olives and flat-leaf parsley sprigs

Preheat broiler. Place all bell peppers in a shallow baking pan and broil until skins are blistered and blackened, turning often to char evenly. Remove peppers from pan, place in a plastic bag and close bag tightly. Let peppers sweat 10 to 15 minutes, then remove and discard skins, stems and seeds. Cut flesh into strips; arrange in a shallow dish. Drizzle oil over peppers. Cut garlic into thin slivers and scatter it over peppers; season with salt and pepper. Cover and let marinate 24 hours. To serve, garnish with olives and parsley sprigs. Makes 4 to 6 servings.

Summer Ratatouille

1 fennel bulb, if available
1/4 cup virgin olive oil
1 large onion, thinly sliced
1 garlic clove, crushed
1 large beefsteak tomato, peeled,
    chopped
1 red bell pepper, seeded, cut into
    squares
1 yellow bell pepper, seeded, cut into
    squares
1 green bell pepper, seeded, cut into
    squares
12 oz. zucchini, sliced
1 teaspoon chopped fresh thyme
Salt and black pepper to taste
1 tablespoon shredded fresh basil

Trim fennel bulb, reserving some of feathery leaves for garnish. Thinly slice bulb. Heat oil in a large saucepan; add fennel slices, onion and garlic. Cover and cook gently 5 minutes. Add tomato and cook 10 minutes longer; add all bell peppers, zucchini, thyme, salt and pepper and cook 5 minutes longer. Remove from heat; let cool. Transfer to a serving dish, sprinkle with basil and garnish with reserved fennel leaves. Makes 6 servings.

Moroccan Sugared Lettuce

1 head Bibb or green leaf lettuce or escarole
1/2 to 2/3 cup pitted dates, cut lengthwise into halves or thirds
3 satsumas, clementines or other tight-skinned mandarin oranges
2 tablespoons superfine sugar
3 tablespoons white wine vinegar
Black pepper to taste

Tear lettuce or escarole into bite-size pieces and place in a salad bowl along with dates. Cut a few thin strips of peel (colored part only) from 1 satsuma or clementine; set aside. Then remove peel from all fruit; cut fruit into slices. Cut slices into smaller pieces and add to lettuce in bowl. Sprinkle with sugar; toss. Sprinkle with vinegar and toss again. Season with pepper. Garnish with reserved strips of peel and serve. Makes 6 servings.

Radish Salad

About 8 oz. daikon
Salt
1 bunch radishes, trimmed, quartered
2 tablespoons sunflower oil
2 teaspoons dark sesame oil
4 teaspoons rice vinegar
1 tablespoon sesame seeds

Peel daikon, then grate or cut into very thin julienne strips. Place on paper towels and sprinkle with salt. Let stand 30 minutes. Squeeze out any excess moisture, then place daikon in a bowl and mix with radishes. Stir together sunflower oil, sesame oil and vinegar; stir into salad. Place salad in a serving bowl, sprinkle with sesame seeds and serve. Makes 6 servings.

—————— Cucumber & Dill Salad ——————

1 large cucumber
Salt
4 teaspoons lemon juice or white wine
    vinegar
Freshly ground black pepper, if desired
1 tablespoon chopped fresh dill

Peel cucumber, cut in half lengthwise and scrape out seeds. Slice crosswise, place in a colander, sprinkle with salt and let stand 30 minutes. Rinse; pat dry on paper towels. Place cucumber slices in a bowl and sprinkle with lemon juice or vinegar. Season with pepper, if desired. Sprinkle with dill and stir to mix. Makes 4 to 6 servings.

Arranged Green Salad

3 oz. snow peas, ends and strings removed
8 oz. fresh asparagus, tough stalk ends
removed
2 medium avocados
Lime & Pistachio Dressing, see below
1/2 bunch watercress, trimmed
About 1 cup alfalfa sprouts

Lime & Pistachio Dressing:
About 1/4 cup shelled pistachio nuts
Grated peel and juice of 1/2 lime
1 tablespoon virgin olive oil
1 tablespoon sunflower oil
Salt and black pepper to taste

Cook snow peas in boiling water 30
seconds; drain and pat dry on paper
towels. Cook asparagus in boiling water
7 to 8 minutes or just until tender.
Drain and let cool. Halve, pit and peel
avocados. Place each half, cut side
down, on a board; slice crosswise.
Transfer each sliced half to a plate and
gently separate slices. Arrange snow
peas along 1 side of avocado, asparagus
down other side. To prepare Lime &
Pistachio Dressing, chop pistachios, if
desired; place in a bowl and stir in
remaining dressing ingredients. Spoon
dressing over salad. Garnish with
watercress and alfalfa sprouts. Makes 4
servings.

Winter Green Salad

2 cups fresh broccoli flowerets
1 head iceberg lettuce
1 bunch watercress, trimmed
1 (about 15-oz.) can artichoke hearts in
    water, drained, halved
1 fennel bulb, trimmed, thinly sliced
1 green bell pepper, seeded, sliced
Green Goddess Dressing, see below

Green Goddess Dressing:
1 recipe Mayonnaise, page 12
2 flat anchovy fillets, drained, finely
    chopped
3 small green onions, finely chopped
2 tablespoons chopped parsley
1 tablespoon tarragon vinegar
1 tablespoon lemon juice
1 garlic clove, crushed
3 tablespoons dairy sour cream
Salt and black pepper to taste

Cook broccoli flowerets in boiling water about 5 minutes or just until bright green and tender-crisp. Drain; let cool. Break lettuce into bite-size pieces and place in a serving bowl along with watercress. Add cooled broccoli, artichokes, fennel and bell pepper. Toss to mix. To prepare Green Goddess Dressing, mix all dressing ingredients (or process in a blender) until well blended. Spoon a little of the dressing over the salad; offer the rest separately. Makes 6 to 8 servings.

Tossed Green Salad

About 10 cups greens of your choice,
such as chicory, escarole, romaine lettuce, Bibb lettuce or iceberg lettuce
(include at least 2 kinds of greens)
Salt
1 garlic clove, peeled
1 tablespoon wine vinegar
1/4 teaspoon Dijon-style mustard
2 teaspoons lemon juice
1/4 cup extra-virgin olive oil
A few young spinach leaves, washed
well, trimmed
1 bunch watercress, trimmed
1/2 cucumber, sliced or diced
1 medium green bell pepper, seeded,
chopped
2 tablespoons chopped mixed fresh
herbs, such as parsley, chervil, tarragon, summer savory or chives

Tear any large leaves of greens into
smaller pieces. If not using immediately, place in a plastic bag and
refrigerate until ready to use. To
assemble salad, put a little salt into a
wooden salad bowl. Add garlic clove;
crush to a paste with salt, using back of a
wooden spoon. Add vinegar, mustard
and lemon juice; stir in oil and continue
to mix to make an emulsion. Add
greens, spinach, watercress, cucumber,
bell pepper and herbs; toss well, so ev-
ery leaf is coated with dressing. Serve
immediately. Makes 6 servings.

TIP: For a less garlicky flavor, rub inside of bowl with a cut garlic clove, then
discard garlic. (If you do not have a
wooden salad bowl, make dressing in a
separate small bowl and pour over salad
just before serving.)

Californian Salad

1 (1/4-oz.) envelope unflavored gelatin
6 tablespoons water
4 teaspoons sugar
2 lemons
3 tablespoons white wine vinegar
A few drops of yellow food coloring, if
  desired
8 oz. fresh asparagus, tough stalk ends
  removed, spears cooked and cooled
2 large carrots, grated
1 large avocado
Fresh dill sprigs

In a small saucepan, sprinkle gelatin over water and let stand about 5 minutes or until spongy. Then stir over low heat until gelatin is dissolved. Stir in sugar; remove from heat and let cool. Grate peel (colored part only) from 1 lemon; place in a 2-quart measure or a bowl. Squeeze juice from both lemons; reserve 1 tablespoon juice and add remainder to peel in 2-quart measure. Add enough cold water to make 3-3/4 cups liquid. Stir in dissolved gelatin, vinegar and, if desired, food coloring. Pour a little of the mixture into a large (7- to 8-cup) ring mold and refrigerate until set. Cut tips off cooked asparagus spears; arrange tips on set gelatin mixture. Chop remainder of spears and place in a bowl; add carrots. Pit, peel and dice avocado; mix with reserved 1 tablespoon lemon juice, then add to asparagus mixture. Stir in remaining gelatin mixture, then spoon into mold. Refrigerate until set. To serve, dip mold up to rim in hot water for a few seconds; invert onto a plate and lift off mold. Garnish with dill sprigs. Makes 8 servings.

Sunshine Salad

12 oz. carrots, cut into julienne strips
1 yellow bell pepper, seeded, cut into
thin strips
1 red bell pepper, seeded, cut into thin
strips
About 3/4 cup whole-kernel corn, thawed
if frozen
Lemon Vinaigrette, see below
1 tablespoon roasted sunflower seeds

Lemon Vinaigrette:
1/4 cup sunflower oil
5 teaspoons lemon juice
1/2 teaspoon Dijon-style mustard
Salt and black pepper to taste

Arrange carrot strips around edge of a shallow bowl or plate. Place yellow and red pepper strips inside this ring in alternate groups. Spoon corn in center. To prepare Lemon Vinaigrette, stir together all vinaigrette ingredients. Drizzle over salad. Sprinkle with sunflower seeds before serving. Makes 6 to 8 servings.

— INDEX —